Sweet Madness

A Love Story
Proving the Power of
Memorizing God's Word

Donna Nicholas

Editing and page design by Ken McFarland
Cover art direction and design by Penny Hall

Copyright © 2002 by Donna Nicholas
Printed in the United States of America
All Rights Reserved

ISBN: 0-9717734-0-8

Contents

Dedication iv
Preface v
Acknowledgments ix
Introduction xi
1. The Call 13
2. Romance 19
3. The Truth 29
4. Studying 35
5. Witnessing 43
6. A Second Call 53
7. A Heavenly Touch 61
8. Memorization 69
9. Growth 77
10. Surrender 91
11. Confrontation 101
12. The First Sheaf 111
13. The Next Sheaves 119
14. The Valley 129
15. The Valley Deepens 139
16. Gethsemane 147
17. Calvary 157
18. Intercession 167
19. Pursuing the Dream 175
20. Waiting 183
21. The Exceeding Abundant Answer 193
22. A Fulfilled Dream 207
23. Epilogue 219

Dedication

To Lori, Tami, and Vonda—the three darling daughters God placed with me to give support in difficult days—and to their husbands and children. May the story in this book be a constant reminder of the power of the memorized Word that gives wings to dreams.

Preface

If you like a love story, you're going to enjoy reading about my love affair with the Lord and my romance with my husband in a marriage that seemed to be made in heaven. My love for my husband can best be described in the words spoken of the early Christians: "They seem to have a sweet madness for Jesus." I truly had a sweet madness for my mate.

Intense love filled my heart, not only for my man, but also for my God—and a passionate dream burned in my breast to work side by side with my husband in shared service for the Lord. I never doubted that ultimately, he would join me to form a team to win many to Christ and His truth. With that aspiration inside, I set myself to seek the Lord to make it happen.

Because I determined to move heaven to fulfill my desires, a marvelous miracle took place. My God introduced me to the power of the memorized Word. As I began hiding His Word in my heart, my love for both my husband and my God grew stronger and stronger. For the first time in my life, I recognized that the Holy

Spirit could make the two of us as powerful as the disciples 2,000 years ago. That thrilling thought turned me more fully to the Word in order to grow spiritually and to claim promises in prayer.

I've told my story openly and honestly, just as I experienced it. As you read of how I sometimes expressed my zeal and fervor, concerns may arise in your mind, but don't leap to any conclusions until you finish the book. You may spot some serious mistakes that I made, but take note that even those bring an encouraging message: Despite the imperfect way we sometimes deal with others and even relate to God, He can still use us to accomplish wonderful and even mighty things for Him. And ultimately, He will find ways not only to help us realize the dreams He places in our hearts, but to get His own perfect will done too.

And that brings me to the most important fact in my story. We know that not all enjoy a fulfilling marriage, but my experience clearly demonstrates that there can be a satisfying love affair that will bring perfect pleasure to every human being. That relationship has been planned and bought from eternity and only awaits our acceptance.

I'm talking about a sweet madness for Jesus. Conditions in our world today reveal that it's time for the love that filled the hearts of the early Christians to be seen again in God's people.

I'm convinced that one powerful way to develop this kind of love is through Scripture memory. In the Word can be found the power to convert, cleanse from sin, and convey the life of Jesus. Those attributes bring a burning love for Him that will fulfill these prophetic words: "The last rays of merciful light, the last message of mercy to be given to the world, is a revelation of His character of love." *Christ's Object Lessons*, page 415.

Scripture memory brings a love for Jesus that gives an eye single to His glory. Be aware of this power in my life as you read my story. Then you can know that the same power that took me through difficult days will carry us all through the time of trouble that faces us in the events soon to break upon our world. Today we must prepare for that day by meditating on the Word day and night. With the Word in our hearts and love for Jesus coursing through our veins, we can stand firm through the last great conflict.

Donna Nicholas
January 2002

Acknowledgments

My special thanks to . . .

Sharon Nottingham, my dear friend who, for years, has encouraged me to write my story.

Mary Coleman, my daughter's friend, who gave help on the first chapters, which encouraged me to continue writing.

Dorrie Philbeck, another friend of whom I asked much advice and who willingly told me what she thought was best.

Dan Vis, the director of FAST Ministries, my faithful friend in Scripture memory who walked with me during stormy days, and as he read my first manuscript, asked several times, "How did you feel when this happened?" When I told him, he replied, "Now write those words in your story to give it more feeling." And I did my best.

Robin Sagel, the librarian at Parkview Adventist

School, for her editing help on the first manuscript, and **Marilyn Morgan**, the English teacher at Weimar Academy, for her editing help on the final draft.

My three daughters, **Lori**, **Tami**, and **Vonda**, who for two years have been e-mailed chapter after chapter for their critique, then have been as perfectly honest as only our children can be: "Yes, Mom, that's good!" "No, Mom, that must be changed!"

Introduction

It is my privilege to write this note of commendation on behalf of this book—*Sweet Madness*, by Donna Nicholas.

A few weeks ago, I attended the Ozark Family Camp Meeting at Gentry, Arkansas, and heard Donna give her presentation on the value of memorizing Scripture. I was amazed to witness so many, both young and old, making commitments to begin at once to make Scripture memorization a definite part of their daily spiritual growth program.

Donna writes her manuscript as her own personal story, which makes her subject come to life, making it especially fascinating to younger readers, in my opinion. She uses her own experience to show how memorizing Scripture has given her power to follow God's way for her life instead of her own.

She shows that Scripture memorization produces power to set "captives free," whether from alcohol, drugs, popularity, money, position, or even from what she considers an especially powerful addiction—that of putting another human being ahead of God.

Donna's presentation comes close to my heart as well, for it was when, as a young man, I was looking for a way to be delivered from evil thoughts, that Elder H. M. S. Richards, Sr. pointed me to the Bible text that changed my life: "Thy Word have I hid in mine heart, that I might not sin against Thee." Psalm 119:11. I took his advice to heart and began memorizing Scripture. Since then, it has been my privilege to spend more than fifty years in active Seventh-day Adventist ministry.

It is my conviction that Donna's book will help prepare many children, young people, and adults for the soon second coming of Christ.

Joseph Espinosa—
    Retired pastor,
    Former General Conference Associate Secretary and General Field Secretary,
    Former president in Dominican Republic

1

The Call

I looked up from the pew of the Methodist church where I sat with my family at a revival meeting and saw what seemed to me like a vision of the Saviour standing above the choir loft. As distinctly as if He were speaking the words aloud, I heard Him call, "I want you to keep the Sabbath day holy, Donna, to show My way to the people."

My 11-year-old heart flooded with an all-consuming love for Jesus. Perhaps the revival atmosphere helped to prepare me for such a positive response. I felt I could go anywhere, do anything, and be whatever my Lord wanted me to be. Waves of joy coursed through my body as I looked toward heaven to reply, "Yes, my Lord. I will keep Sunday holy. I will live fully for You." I stood with the congregation to sing with all my heart the closing hymn:

Just as I am, without one plea,
But that Thy blood was shed for me,
And that Thou bid'st me come to Thee,
O Lamb of God, I come, I come.

That dramatic call came in response to a message that had filled my mind for three years—a need to keep the fourth commandment, to make Sunday a sacred day. The desire was planted in my mind after first reading the novel, *Elsie Dinsmore*, by Martha Finley, which I had pulled from the shelves of our small rural school library. Elsie, a devout 8 year old, kept Sunday as the holy Sabbath day. She endured continual harassment from her family for this practice, in addition to ridicule for her meek Christ-like spirit. I read the book many times, with tears of sympathy for Elsie streaming from my eyes. With each reading, my desire grew stronger to be an "Elsie" in Sunday-keeping and Christian living in my own community.

Not only did I read the book, but I checked Bible references the author quoted to make certain it was necessary to keep Sunday. I especially remember reading Isaiah 58:13: "If thou turn away thy foot from the Sabbath, from doing thy pleasure on My holy day . . ." Those words left no doubt in my mind that God commands His day to be kept holy. I realized that the members of my church, including my own family, didn't obey this commandment.

At the close of the service I climbed in the back seat of our old Chevy beside my brother and sisters to ride the seven miles of bumpy western Oklahoma dirt roads to our humble farmhouse. There in the upstairs bedroom I shared with my two sisters, I jumped into bed to dream of my great work. I imagined myself a devout Sabbath-keeper who on Sunday refused to play secular music on the piano or read worldly books. The sweet, Christ-like spirit possessed by Elsie lived in me. I gloried in the fact that I, a young girl, could be mighty for the Lord.

The Call 15

A test the following Sunday brought my dream to stark reality. Grandparents, aunts, uncles, and cousins gathered at our house to spend the day. Family gatherings took place often in our home, and my siblings and I loved these special times. On Saturday we willingly cleaned house, drew extra water from the cistern, and helped with food preparation. Since I loved to put the living room in top order, my responsibility included mopping and waxing the linoleum in that room, plus helping Mom dress and clean three chickens for the dinner.

My brother drove my two sisters and me to church, and then we came home to the excitement of the company. My 11-year-old cousin Dolores and I were inseparable whenever we got together. After Mom's delicious fried chicken dinner with Aunt Maxine's coconut cake for dessert, the men and young people went to the south field for our usual ballgame. As I walked happily beside Dolores, an unwelcome thought entered, *"A Sabbathkeeper shouldn't play ball on Sunday!"*

My commitment flashed before me, bringing tremors from head to toe. "How can I tell my family I can't play ball? My cousins will think I'm strange." Turmoil raged in my breast, driving away all excitement. I quietly moved to stand behind home plate, hoping to be unseen. In misery, I wished the ground would swallow me.

Daddy, waiting his turn to bat, asked me, "Why aren't you playing ball?" Summoning all my courage, I meekly replied, "I don't believe in playing ball on Sunday." My sweet daddy, who rarely said a cross word to any of us, simply turned back to the game. Others who heard paid no attention.

With my commitment now made known, the next logical step took shape in my mind. "I shouldn't be at a ball game on Sunday. Sabbath is a day to spend time with Jesus." Feeling all alone in the world, I turned away from the happy ballplayers to trudge to the house. The weight on my shoulders made walking difficult.

Slipping past the women sitting in the living room, I went to my parents' bedroom. I longed to throw myself on the bed to cry, but I knew I must be strong. Holding back tears, I took my parents' Bible from the dresser and lay down on the bed to attempt to read.

"Donna, what's the matter?" Aunt Rosalie asked as she and my mother came into the bedroom. "Why are you in here reading the Bible while everybody plays ball?"

"I don't believe in playing ball on Sunday." I sat up, tears streaming down my cheeks.

"Honey, Jesus doesn't want you to miss the ball game." My aunt sat on the bed and placed her arm around me. "It's all right to have fun on Sunday. You don't have to sit with your nose in the Bible."

"I believe Sunday is God's Sabbath day which He commands to be kept holy."

My words were scarcely audible as I sniffled and wiped tears from my eyes.

"There are things we shouldn't do on Sunday, but it's not a sin to play ball." Mother added her counsel as she reached into her dresser drawer for a handkerchief and handed it to me. "Dry your eyes, sweetheart. We don't want a sad girl on this happy day."

Tears fell like rain while I thought about the words my

mom and aunt spoke. Then my aunt took the handkerchief and wiped my eyes. I smiled at her, stood to my feet, and without a word followed them into the living room.

"Donna, I want to hear some music," my dear grandmother requested. She loved to hear me play the piano, and in the fashion my daddy loved—"music I can tap my foot to"—I immediately sat down to begin my rendition of "The Tennessee Waltz." The secular song, played on the Sunday Sabbath, effectively erased conviction from my heart. "It's simply too complicated to keep Sabbath," I thought to myself as the beat of the waltz lifted the burden from my shoulders.

From that day, I dismissed all thoughts of keeping Sunday holy; however, I didn't forsake the Lord. At the end of that week I knelt behind my bedroom door to plead forgiveness for failure to obey my mother. The cleansing floods of heaven washed me clean, bringing such intense love for Jesus that I again felt a burning zeal to make my life count wholly for Him.

2

Romance

Besides my love for the Lord, another interest came into my life when I was only 12 years old. In seventh grade, the seating arrangement placed my desk beside that of Duane, an eighth grader, who loved to tease. One day I memorized the third paragraph of the Gettysburg Address: "Now we're engaged in a great Civil War . . ." I looked up to see big green eyes winking at me. Embarrassed, I repeated the words three times: "Now we're engaged . . . now we're engaged . . . now we're engaged."

Another eighth grader spoke up: "Duane and Donna are engaged!" My face flushed, and I hung my head, but a warm, fuzzy feeling filled my heart. That tall, lanky almost-13-year-old suddenly became the most handsome guy in the world to me. Taking an instant liking to me, he kidded me incessantly. Even at his young age, he possessed all the self-confidence that I lacked, which drew me to him like a magnet. I laughed at his witty remarks. My eyes carefully followed his every move on the basketball court and on the baseball diamond. I reveled in the fact that students of every age loved to be around him.

My dream to exalt the way of God now gained new proportions—"Duane and I will do a great work for the Lord," I determined. Since young people from the seventh grade through the twelfth grade were in the youth class in Sunday School, Duane and I sat in this classroom every Sunday morning. The magnitude of my dream increased one week as our teacher presented "The Call," a motivating lesson on Methodist young people called of God to witness door to door about their Christian walk. I hoped Duane and I might be involved in this exciting mission, but the plan never materialized in our church.

However, my spiritual life gained success in the Sunday night Methodist Youth Fellowship meetings, which Duane and I began to attend this same year. Since my mother and teachers had encouraged me from childhood to present memorized readings and poetry, I immediately led out in presenting lessons for the youth group. I made up my own presentations—memorized portions of articles in magazines such as *Christian Herald*, Billy Graham's newsletter, and other religious material that came in our mail. When I led up front, I loved seeing Duane's eyes on me, feeding my hope that he also realized we had a future in the work of God.

Two years later, my speaking career took a step forward when I performed a reading entitled "The County Fair" at a talent show at a nearby school. I did a dramatic rendition of the people seen at the county fair—the barker, the flirt, the spoiled child, and the old couple. To my amazement, I won first place in readings, giving me the privilege of making the same presentation on the radio station in Clinton, a nearby city.

The attention made me feel like a movie star, a sentiment enhanced within a few days when Duane asked me to go to a party with him at the superintendent's home. It was the end of my freshman year. For three years my feelings had smoldered. Now they ignited into a flame as he took me in his parents' car on my first date. Mom made me a new dress for the occasion. We played Rook, talked, laughed, and ate refreshments. It seemed like my coronation as princess as I sat beside the good-looking president of the sophomore class. At the end of the evening, I jumped into bed to dream that I could be the sweetheart forever of this wonderful guy.

Dating now became a regular part of my life, with our weekly attendance at the Methodist Youth Fellowship meetings. Then, just ten months after our first engagement and shortly before my sixteenth birthday, I experienced a broken heart. Duane called one Sunday afternoon to ask me to attend a movie with him and another couple. I turned from the phone to ask Mom if I could go. She said, "It seems to me that young people could find something better to do on Sunday than go to a movie."

I immediately remembered the broken Sunday-keeping covenant I had made with the Lord several years earlier. Without even pleading with my mother, I replied, "I can't go." Much to my sorrow, Duane asked another girl to go with him, temporarily ending our relationship. I was crushed. Time healed my broken heart, but I continued to think sweet thoughts about Duane and resolved that someday I would make him mine again.

On a happy day in August, five months later, the young people stood outside talking after our Sunday night meeting. Duane casually walked to my side and spoke softly so others couldn't hear: "I'd like to take you home tonight."

My heart skipped a beat. "I'll ask my brother if he thinks my parents would allow me to go."

My brother gave me permission, so Duane and I drove away together. Immediately he apologized for dating the other girl. "I don't know why I went with her so long. I really wanted to go with you."

The five months of separation vanished from my mind, and we talked nonstop all the way home. I knew I should play hard to get, but my happiness obliterated such thoughts. His new maturity made me feel so special. My heart filled with love for him, and I walked into the house with starry eyes.

Our relationship now became serious. We began to have Saturday night dates in addition to our attendance at the Sunday night Methodist Youth Fellowship. On one occasion, we got into the car after a Roy Rogers' movie. As he drove me home, we talked about the show. Then suddenly, without looking at me, he surprised me with his words: "Oh, Donna, I love you!"

Thrilled, yet embarrassed, I blurted unthinkingly, "How do you know? You're not very old."

Duane didn't say another word all the way home. After he shut off the engine, he quietly said, "I wish I hadn't told you that."

Innocently, I asked, "What do you wish you hadn't told me?"

Romance 23

"I wish I hadn't told you that I loved you." Then he turned from his place behind the wheel to look straight at me. "But I do love you. Tell me, do you love me?"

My shyness melted away. "Yes, Duane, I love you." I slipped into his outstretched arms. He knew I loved him. I had loved him since I was 12 years old. That fact soon became obvious to my family, my friends, and my teachers. They even seemed to smile on our relationship in spite of our youth.

About this time I determined to write a special program for the youth meeting. I searched my Bible, finally settling on the Sermon on the Mount. Again, I memorized the verses, repeating them while I sat in my room and as I brought in the milk cows each evening. Soon I stood in front of the young people quoting "Blessed are the poor in spirit, for theirs is the kingdom of heaven." Matthew 5:3. The pride in Duane's eyes brought the familiar thought to my mind, "Surely, he knows that Jesus has a special plan for us."

The verses I had hidden in my heart made my love for the Lord burn brighter than ever, renewing my desire to point people to Him in a living relationship. I longed to devote my whole life to Jesus, but I also wanted Duane by my side. I knew I should talk to him about our religious convictions, but his apparent spiritual indifference made me reluctant to mention the subject.

Finally on one of his Sunday afternoon visits as we sat together on a bench in our yard, I boldly asked, "Why do you think we experience strong feelings for people, but we don't sense deep love for God?"

Duane kicked a rock from beside his foot before he answered me. "Love for God is a very personal matter.

Perhaps it should be labeled respect or awe instead of love."

His answer disappointed me, so I told him my thoughts. "I think we should love God just as we love people. He wants us to have a relationship with Him that will make attending church, reading the Word, and being obedient enjoyable activities instead of formal duties."

"Well, I don't know how to describe my love for God, but I know that I don't have the same kind of feeling for Him that I have for you." Duane placed his arm around my shoulders and lifted my chin with his other hand. "You think more about God than anyone I know, but maybe that's one of the reasons I love you."

Since we didn't agree, I dropped the subject. In my heart, though, I knew I was right—God wants a love from His people that gives them a desire to please Him. Since Duane didn't appear to have the same opinion, I refused to talk about spiritual goals in his presence. My love for the Lord and my love for my man seemed like two separate fires burning in my heart, which could be united only in my dreams.

Following my graduation from high school, Duane came to visit with surprising news. "I've got something special to tell you. Let's go outdoors." The stars twinkled from a beautiful sky as we walked hand in hand to the pasture behind the house. He stopped, and taking both my hands in his, turned to face me: "My aunt and uncle leave tomorrow to go home to Kalamazoo, Michigan, and they want me to go with them. My aunt can get me a job at Shakespeare Fishing Rod and Reel Company, where she works, and I can continue college."

I caught my breath as I tried to comprehend the idea of him leaving. "Oh! I can't bear to think of you living way up there."

He pulled me close to him. "With a good job, I can pay my school bill and buy a car. If I have a vehicle of my own and a little money, you and I can get married next summer. What do you think of that?"

"You're proposing to me!" I exclaimed, goose bumps breaking out all over. "We've never seriously talked about marriage, but you know there's nothing I want so much as to be your wife."

"That's the reason I need to go to Michigan. I can't find a good-paying job near the college in Weatherford, but the money I can make in the north paves the way for us to have an easier life together."

"I know you're right, but I don't know if I can stand a year without you."

Thoughts of our future happiness placed a request on my lips. "God is so good to you and me. Pray for us, Duane."

He spoke a simple prayer: "Father, thank You for giving Donna to me. Take care of the two of us these next few months while we separate. Please make our marriage plans come true. Amen."

A few days later we said a sad goodbye. Duane went to Michigan to live with his aunt and uncle, work at Shakespeare, and begin his second year of college at Western Michigan College in Kalamazoo. I moved to live with my aunt and uncle in Weatherford, where I found a job as a night telephone operator and started my first year of college. We exchanged letters daily, but I could hardly wait for the year to pass so we could be married.

All that year, I read my Bible daily and attended church faithfully, but plans for my work for Jesus faded in comparison to thoughts of married life. I saw couples who seemed to have no affection for each other, and I vowed my marriage would be different. I would keep our love affair alive. I had intense feeling for this one who was outstanding in every area of his life except for his spiritual strength, and I knew that could come with my encouragement.

The school year passed. Then one sultry, late-June day, as I sat at my machine sewing wedding clothes, I heard a knock. Startled, I opened the door to see my tall, handsome man standing before me. "I didn't expect you until tomorrow," I cried, as I fell into his outstretched arms.

"I couldn't wait to get here. I drove the whole 1,100 miles without stopping to sleep."

"I'm so sad you caught me in such a mess," I lamented. "I spend every free minute sewing and take no time to fix my hair."

"I don't call you a mess." He held me away to look me over. "You're the prettiest girl I've seen since I left Oklahoma."

The wedding took place on Sunday, July 18, 1954, in our Methodist Church. I donned the dress I had made, a princess-style pattern of white taffeta with sparkly trim woven all through the fabric. It fit my waist, then billowed into a full circle at the hemline, which fell about three inches above my ankles. I wanted a street-length dress so I could wear it to festive occasions in the future.

I placed the cap with attached veil on my head, and confidently walked to the foot of the stairs at 2:00 to listen to the piano music.

My little sister Peggy and a neighbor boy lit the candles. After walking down the aisle with my dad, I took Duane's arm, and we stood for the ceremony with my sister Lois and Duane's friend as our attendants. Our youth fellowship sponsor sang love songs, then read, "How Do I Love Thee?" by Elizabeth Barrett Browning. When she began, Duane and I turned to make it appear that we were speaking the beautiful words to each other: "*I love thee to the depth and breadth and height my soul can reach.*"

We made our vows to cherish each other till death—words that seemed unnecessary in view of our strong affection. Nothing could come between the two of us. We were childhood sweethearts whose feelings had deepened as our lives matured, and now we truly loved to the depths of our beings. Such devotion was destined to last forever.

3

The Truth

Our married life began in a small apartment in Kalamazoo, Michigan, 1,100 miles from home. I found a job as a secretary, while Duane continued his part-time work and college studies. True to our farm backgrounds of eating big breakfasts, I cooked the bacon and eggs three mornings of the week, and he prepared the food the other two days. On weekends we bought groceries, cooked, did the laundry, and visited friends. Because there was no Sunday School class for married couples our age, the Methodist church made us assistants to the teachers of the junior high class. I felt gratified to be involved in the work of God, while both Duane and I enjoyed the admiration of youth only a few years younger than ourselves.

From the beginning of our lives together, I depended on my husband. He managed our money and efficiently took care of all business. He made such wise choices that I soon learned never to make a decision without consulting him. Daily, our lives entwined to make us better friends and sweeter lovers.

After two years in Kalamazoo, Duane graduated with an education degree, and we moved to Galien, Michigan, where he would teach junior high math and coach basketball in the Galien public schools. Now that I no longer needed to work to help with our living expenses, I determined to become a teacher also. We drove to Berrien Springs, eighteen miles away, so I could schedule classes at Emmanuel Missionary College, a Seventh-day Adventist institution.

"I never heard of people keeping the seventh day of the week for a Sabbath," I remarked to Duane as we got into the car to return to our home after my enrollment.

"It seems a little strange," he agreed, "but I know the Bible calls the seventh day the Sabbath. If Christians use the Bible for their guide, then these people would be right."

"I have thought Sunday was God's special day since childhood," I replied. "The worship day must have been changed to Sunday, and the Seventh-day Adventists don't recognize the new day." I didn't mention my childhood experience in Sunday-keeping.

The next day brought a big surprise as I donned my pretty blue dress with matching jewelry, painted my mouth a fiery red, and headed for the college. I reported to the registrar's office to see about work.

Dr. Rasmussen, the registrar, was a small Danish man who seemed quite interested in the fact that I had chosen to attend his school. "I see by your application that you belong to the Methodist church. It might interest you to know that many of the founders of our faith were Methodists, so we share a common bond." He looked at me kindly, then said, "We don't care what church you belong to, but you must understand that you won't be able to wear your jewelry or makeup on this campus. Will that be a problem?"

Though shocked, I hastened to say, "Oh, that won't matter to me." I hoped the answer satisfied him, because I couldn't imagine myself without makeup. Jewelry wasn't important, but I felt naked without lipstick.

"I can give you about twelve hours of work in this office each week," he continued. "Your job will be to type copies of students' transcripts, so you can choose your hours."

Thrilled at this good news, I could hardly wait to get home to tell Duane. The $250 tuition per semester at this private school seemed incredibly high to us, but my salary would more than pay the cost.

In the following days I sat in class and worked in the office with girls who wore no outward adornment. It amazed me that the boys seemed to like their plain appearance. The men in my world wanted makeup on women. I felt perfectly natural at school, but at the end of the day, when I got in my car, I immediately smeared lipstick on my lips.

As the weeks passed, a great uneasiness arose in my heart. On this campus, I seemed to have returned to my days of reading *Elsie Dinsmore*. Like Elsie, young people here openly talked about their relationship with the Lord, calling Him their best friend. Youth led in prayer and religious discussions and pursued goals to become church school teachers, ministers, and missionaries—the same aspirations I had as a child.

Since our marriage, Duane and I had continued to attend church faithfully every Sunday, and in our church in Galien, we had immediately become sponsors of the youth group. However, I no longer identified with the conservative ideas of my girlhood. I stood beside my husband, conforming to the standards of the world, while we practiced diligent church work.

My uneasiness drove me to complain to Duane. "These Adventists are just too much! They don't allow movies, smoking or drinking, not even caffeine drinks. They don't eat meat. In fact, one of my friends in biology class told me that she had never tasted meat and wouldn't think of eating it. Can you imagine real people living like this?"

"It surely wouldn't be a life for me, but if it makes them happy, let them live that way," Duane answered.

Then I found a verse that brought comfort: "Let no man therefore judge you in meat, or in drink, or in respect of an holyday, or of the new moon, or of the Sabbath days." Colossians 2:16. Those words proved to me that it wasn't necessary to keep the seventh-day Sabbath. In spite of my determination to think no more about it, uneasiness about my faith continued to plague my thoughts.

A few weeks later I asked my Methodist pastor for help with a talk for my speech class. He listened as I described the standards practiced on the campus. "Adventists plan all week for activities which enable them to keep the Sabbath holy. The church forbids anything considered worldly, although it seems some slip away to attend movies and dances. I need your help to write a speech proving that it's a relationship with Christ that makes faith real."

Pastor Bill spoke with perfect confidence. "Seventh-day Adventists teach works, which have nothing to do with salvation. Salvation comes through grace and is given to us free. I choose to smoke in order to demonstrate to my flock that we can be saved without any works of the law." His shocking words made it difficult for me to keep a straight face. I had no idea my pastor smoked and felt horrified to hear him openly confess it.

I left his office with the contrast between my liberal Methodist church and the conservative Adventist church glaringly revealed. Since I couldn't imagine changing membership, I threw myself into work to upgrade my church. No Sunday School class for young adults existed, so I organized and taught a class for this age. Duane seemed proud of my religious zeal. He didn't join in the visitation, but he sat in the group every Sunday actively participating.

All my good works couldn't extinguish the flame of feelings burning in my heart. I sensed the same dissatisfaction with my spiritual life that had plagued me as a child. At that time, God had shown me His way in a novel about a dedicated Christian girl. Now about ten years later, He was revealing His way in the lives of real people. Their confidence spoke of their knowledge that they walked in truth. I knew that assurance came from making the Bible their guideline, not only in Sabbath-keeping, but in every area of their lives.

How I longed to live that kind of life! But now, as in my childhood, I faced many obstacles. The greatest hindrance was my love for my husband, who had no interest, although he admitted that it was right. He and I walked in perfect harmony. I loved him too much to consider any step that didn't include him.

Love for the world brought another difficulty. While I longed to belong fully to the Lord, it brought me great fulfillment to be the wife of a teacher and basketball coach. Cheering his team to victory at the basketball games thrilled my heart. Social times with the other teachers—drinking colas and talking about games and school activities—became highlights of my life. And I wondered how there could be any fun for a people who couldn't even play competitive sports.

So with mixed emotions in my heart, I left the Adventist campus at the end of the year. In spite of all the problems involved, as we headed south, a tiny flame in my heart brought a new thought, "Some day, I must be a Seventh-day Adventist."

4

Studying

"These Bible Story books prove invaluable in the character development of children." Alma Kerbs, a literature evangelist, turned the pages of several books as she pointed to stories illustrating certain traits while Duane and I listened attentively.

She had come to our home in response to a lead card I had mailed only two weeks before. I was sitting in the doctor's office with our girls, 3-year-old Lori and 3-month-old Tami, when Lori handed me the sample copy of *The Bible Story* from the table in front of us with her usual request, "Read to me, Mommy." From my year on the campus of Emmanuel Missionary College, I recognized the book as one of the ten-volume set sold by Seventh-day Adventist literature evangelists. I began to read, sensing a strong impression that this reading material would teach Lori and Tami to love Jesus.

Impulsively, I wrote my name and address on the card in the back of the book, then stopped at the post office on the way home to mail it. A feeling of happiness flooded my soul—I sensed I had taken a giant step toward God.

Now as Alma made her presentation, I desperately wanted *The Bible Story* for our home. Duane held back to ask the all-important question, "What is the price of this set?"

"Only $110.00."

"$110.00!" Duane exclaimed, as if he were shocked. "That's way too much! I don't want your books." His words sounded final.

Since he showed no interest, Alma turned to me. "Would *you* like to have these books?"

"Yes, but my husband is the breadwinner, so I leave the decision to him." I smiled sweetly at Duane.

Alma again reminded Duane of the well-written stories and the durability of the paper and covers. "Our books are the finest quality in every way."

He ignored every argument. "I'm sorry, but you haven't convinced me that the value of your books equals the price you ask for them. My answer is no."

My disappointment knew no bounds, but I knew Duane wouldn't change his mind. Yearning to tell her about my experience with Seventh-day Adventists, I changed the subject, "Five years ago I attended your college in Berrien Springs, where I worked in the registrar's office and took classes for two semesters."

Alma immediately showed great interest in the fact that I had attended an Adventist college, asking several questions: "Why did you choose Emmanuel Missionary College? What subjects did you study? What did you think of Seventh-day Adventists?"

The sparkle in my eyes when I talked about life on the

campus must have eased her regret in not making a sale.

She stood to leave, then announced, "A Christian home like yours should have *The Bible Story*. When I come to this area again, I'll stop by."

She left, and Duane shut the door behind her. Placing my hands on my hips, I turned on him immediately. "Just why wouldn't you buy the books? They would teach our girls to be good and love Jesus. Don't you think we need them?" Tears of distress stung my eyes.

"Perhaps the books would be valuable to the girls, but I refuse to pay a fortune for them, no matter how good they may be," Duane countered. He sat down and pulled me onto his lap. "Don't look so sad. You can buy them when she returns. Why should we make life easy for her?"

"Oh, Duane, you're such a case! I love you so much, even though you have to be the craziest guy in the whole world." I threw my arms around him. "I'm so glad that you want the books, too! I can't wait for her to come."

Within weeks, Mrs. Kerbs returned, and I gave her a check for *The Bible Story*. She assured me the books would come in the mail soon, along with the *New Life* Bible correspondence course from the Voice of Prophecy. After praying with me, she left. My heart felt unusually light and joyful with the knowledge that the books and Bible study linked me to God's special people again.

It had been five years since Duane and I had left Michigan to return to Oklahoma, where he continued his career in education as the high school principal and junior high coach in Dill City public schools. I drove to Weatherford to complete my degree in business education, taught fifth and sixth grade in Dill City for two years, then to my great satisfaction became a full-time housewife. The birth of our two daughters added a wonderful dimension to our family happiness. Again, as in Michigan, we became quite active in our Methodist church, where we taught Sunday School classes, sponsored the youth group, and participated in every church activity.

My interest in speaking blossomed, now that I no longer worked outside my home. An inner desire for God drove me to the religious section of the library to find books for my programs, both for my church and in the community. I presented *A New Song* by Pat Boone, *Time Out, Ladies* by Dale Evans, and *The Day Christ Died* by Jim Bishop. These books appealed to me because each one emphasized an intimate walk with Jesus. Again, as in my youth, I typed and memorized the author's own words in each presentation.

Another source I used for lessons in my women's organization at church and in the youth group was *These Times* magazine—a gift sent to me from the time we left Michigan by an anonymous donor. I devoured every issue, fueling the desire for Sabbath-keeping still hidden in my heart.

The Bible Story books came in the mail a few days later. I sat down immediately to read to the girls. But the blessing on that day didn't compare to the expectancy in my heart almost two weeks later when the first two lessons of the *New Life* correspondence course arrived in the mail. My hungry soul absorbed every word as I completed the answer sheets and mailed them the next day.

It seemed like an eternity before the next lessons came, but this time I was thrilled to find four studies in the pack. In one day I read all of them, worked the answer sheets and sent them back. The beauty of these simple, basic Bible truths stirred my heart. I accepted each teaching without question, then listed all texts under the subject headings in the blank pages of my Bible and underlined the verses in red.

From the time the first studies came, I shared them with Duane. Happiness overflowed within me as he attentively listened and made a few comments. He and I had enjoyed perfect communication in every area of our lives except in religion, and now we shared in spiritual discussions. As the weeks passed, we began understanding subjects we knew little about—the second coming, the millennium, heaven, and tithing. Since the day I had mailed the interest card, the desire of my girlhood to do a work for Jesus had come fully back to life. Now that Duane and I were studying truths of the Word, I felt we were being prepared for our future work. Since the lessons were the stimulus for our spiritual growth, they couldn't come fast enough to please me.

Several weeks later, after supper, I quickly cleared the table. The girls played happily in the living room. Anticipating a step nearer to the Lord, I placed my hand on my husband's shoulder. "Keep your place, Duane. I have something to show you." I brought my Bible with the study material that had come in the mail that day and held them before him. "Can you believe all four of these lessons are on the Sabbath? They cover every question on the subject anyone could possibly ask. They leave no doubt that the Sabbath commandment means we're to keep the seventh day holy." My enthusiasm poured forth in a glowing report.

Very calmly, Duane responded, "I don't need to read

these lessons to know that the seventh day is the Sabbath. I've thought that for a long time."

"I know you have, but there are many people who don't believe it. We need to read these arguments for the Sabbath so we can know how to convince them."

"I have no plans to convince anybody, because I really don't care," Duane replied.

Disappointment edged into my heart, but I kept it carefully hidden. Duane just *had* to realize the importance of the Sabbath, and I knew the studies were the best way to teach him. I pointed to the first paper. "These words show that God's law is a perfect law. It has existed from eternity, even though most people think the law went into effect with the Ten Commandments."

"You've learned these lessons quickly," Duane answered. "Perhaps these people need to hire you to work for them."

"Duane, be serious. This is important." I placed another study in front of him. "Do you realize that God didn't change the seventh-day Sabbath to Sunday? People made the change many years ago."

"I thought our church observed Sunday because Jesus rose from the dead on the first day of the week," he said.

"That's right." I thanked God under my breath that he appeared more serious.

"This lesson makes clear that Sunday is mentioned only eight times in the New Testament, and not one of those times gives it sacredness. It seems impossible, but what the majority of churches teach is wrong."

"You're not telling me anything new, Donna. I be-

Studying 41

lieve the Sabbath is the seventh day." He rose from his chair, pushed it back into position, and turned to go. "I have things to do besides study your lessons."

"No! You can't go." I stood in front of him to block his path. I just couldn't stand for him to leave before we finished.

"You need a little more size if you intend to keep me here." He pushed me aside, laughing as he walked to the garage.

I placed my lessons and Bible back on the coffee table, then prayed as I returned to the sink of dirty dishes. "Father, Duane and I both believe this wonderful truth. Please send conviction upon him. I know Your hand rests upon us, because You have great plans for us to show the Sabbath truth to Your world. With all my heart, that's what I want to do. Hasten Your work in my husband."

5

Witnessing

"You're early today. Have you eaten breakfast?" My mother-in-law turned from her stove to look at our family of four as we walked into their family room on Saturday morning.

"No, we haven't eaten. Hope we're not too late to get a little food here." Duane sat in the chair opposite his dad, holding Tami on his lap.

"You know better than that," she chided. "Donna, will you please set the table and make toast and orange juice? I'll cook some more bacon, fry the eggs, and we'll have breakfast in just a few minutes. How are my granddaughters?" She smiled lovingly at the girls.

"I'm fine, Grandma." Lori ran to give her grandma a hug, then added, "But I'm not very hungry for an egg."

"She can eat cold cereal, Mom. You know this daughter of ours doesn't like eggs."

I placed plates and silverware on the table and pushed the bread down in the toaster. Soon we sat around the table to enjoy a typical breakfast at the farm. After we ate, Duane and his dad took Lori and went to check on a water well pump. I happily watched them walk out the door, giving me the private time with my mother-in-law that I desired. Today I had determined to inform both my mother-in-law and my mother about the Bible study truths.

I had almost completed the correspondence course and had shared every teaching with Duane. He had agreed with me that the doctrines presented were in agreement with the Bible: the sleeping state of the dead, the ultimate annihilation of the wicked, the importance of the Sabbath in daily living and in prophetic teaching, and the health message to abstain from unclean meat and caffeine. We recognized that these teachings made perfect sense. It seemed impossible that so many churches, including our own, taught false doctrines. I longed to become a Seventh-day Adventist. Even though Duane seemed to have no interest, his acceptance of the beliefs gave me confidence that conviction would soon touch both of us to become members of that church. Since we maintained a close relationship with our parents, who both lived about forty miles from Dill City on the same farms where they had lived all their lives, I knew they must be informed.

As we began to clear the table, I asked, "Mom, do you remember that I attended an Adventist college in Michigan?"

"Yes, I recall that you held their school in high regard."

"Yes, I did." I turned on the faucets to run dishwater, then continued, "I've been taking a correspondence Bible study sponsored by an Adventist organization. Duane

Witnessing 45

studies with me, and we're astonished by how closely their teaching follows the Bible."

"It's certainly good that you're studying the Bible together," my mother-in-law responded. She and I had been as close as a mother and daughter since Duane's and my marriage.

"The Seventh-day Adventist Church proclaims Saturday to be the Sabbath." As soon as I made this statement, I hurried on to ease the shock of my words. "We've been surprised to discover that the Bible teaches this truth. The fourth commandment, which requires the day to be kept holy, remains in effect."

"Are you and Duane going to become Sabbath-keepers?" Concern was written all over my mother-in-law's face.

"Oh, no! We both believe in the Sabbath, but Duane isn't at all interested in changing churches." I wanted to tell her that I thought we would soon be taking that step, but her response made me decide to wait for a better time.

Then I brought up a different doctrine: "The teaching of this correspondence course on the subject of hell has been a real eye opener to us. Countless verses in the Bible prove that hell is a fire that burns up—not a fire that burns forever as most churches teach."

"What an interesting thought," she said. "I think the Bible plainly teaches that the fires of hell burn throughout eternity."

"A casual reading of the Bible seems to say that, but listen to this verse: 'The day that cometh shall burn them up, that it shall leave them neither root nor branch'

[Malachi 4:1]. Notice that it says they're burned up, not continually burning. Many other verses state the same fact. If you were to read through this Bible study, you could never believe that God plans to burn sinners throughout eternity. This awful doctrine presents God as a sadist who enjoys seeing people suffer. I can't believe most churches believe and teach such a dogma."

Before my mother-in-law could answer, Duane, Lori, and his dad entered the house, and Duane said to me, "We need to go, Donna. I have lots of work to do at your folks' place."

"I'll tell you more another time, Mom," I said, drying my hands and picking up Tami, who had been sitting on the floor playing.

"Just what are you telling my mom this time?" Duane asked, as we climbed into the pickup and he steered east.

"Wouldn't you like to know?" I teased, and then to change the subject, I asked, "Is the pump working?"

I was elated at my success in sharing the truths of the Bible with my mother-in-law. She and my father-in-law took great pride in Duane's work as a principal and coach in the Dill City public schools and in our active life in the community. I sensed that a change would bring them sadness, but there was no place in my heart to think about any problems involved. I allowed my mind to dwell only on positive thoughts of our future as Seventh-day Adventists during the drive to my parent's farm.

Since our second year in Dill City, Duane had partnered with my daddy in a cattle operation on their farm. He enjoyed this weekend change from teaching to feeding and checking cattle, repairing fences, and buying feed.

Witnessing 47

The days away from town on the wide open spaces of the farm became special. Often our siblings visited, providing happy family times.

Just as I had shared the Bible lessons with my mother-in-law, I felt equally eager to tell my own mother. The opportunity came quickly as Duane and my dad left to do outside chores. Mother and I went to the kitchen to cook dinner.

Again I broached the subject by telling about the correspondence course. When I presented to my mother the sleeping state of the dead, I was amazed to hear her say, "Honey, your daddy has always told me that when a person dies, he's dead. He doesn't think there's a separate spirit that goes to heaven or hell. Because of his influence, I believe it, too, even though the church teaching disagrees."

"How wonderful, Mom!" I exclaimed, thrilled with her acceptance of such a controversial doctrine. Her positive response spurred me on, but she quickly became negative when I told her about the Sabbath.

"They may seem to be right, honey," she acknowledged, "but I can't really think that a day makes any difference to God. Everybody around here worships on Sunday, and it would be pretty difficult to change to Saturday."

A pang of disappointment tried to crowd away my joy, but I allowed no feelings of defeat. I realized it was best to drop the subject for the time. I continued helping my mother prepare dinner, but our conversation turned to family members and community happenings.

As the sun set, we started home with another satisfying day at the farm behind us. The two conversations with our mothers had made it an extra special day for me. I had no thoughts of the difficulties Sabbath-keeping would bring when, instead of a day at the farm, Saturday would become a day at church. My mind overflowed with thoughts of how we could lead our wonderful Methodist family to accept the Sabbath truth.

Truth had erupted in my heart, and long before the day at the farm I had begun to share my new faith with any listener. In almost every contact of more than a few minutes, I broached the subject of religion. Many of my friends merely tolerated my conversation, but I had discovered real interest in seven of the women I talked to. With them, I started a Bible study on Tuesday mornings in my home using the *New Life* material. All seemed to enjoy the lessons, even when there was a difference of opinion. I gladly led out, anticipating friends uniting with us in this special church.

Soon after the Saturday at the farm, two of my friends stayed behind after our Bible study in which we had discussed the state of the dead and the annihilation of the wicked. Mary surprised me with her frank remark, "You're being drawn into a cult, Donna. If we teach people that God doesn't punish in a forever burning hell, no one will choose to serve Him. Hell is nothing to fear if it ends in a short time and we cease to exist."

Sally interrupted our conversation with a suggestion, "Go with us to the revival meeting at our Nazarene church in Elk City tomorrow night. Brother Wheeler speaks powerfully. It would be good for you to hear him."

"Oh, yes, that would be great! Please go with us." Mary looked at me expectantly.

Witnessing 49

"If Duane will keep the girls, I will," I promised. I had no desire to go, but I reminded myself that they came to my house each week to study the Voice of Prophecy lessons, so perhaps I should show interest in the teaching of their church. Consequently, the following night I sat in the Nazarene church beside my two friends. I felt certain they had talked to the evangelist about me because his message was based on the subject of hell.

"Friends," he addressed the congregation in a concerned voice, "I can't let this time pass without giving you a fair warning of your eternity without God. At this very moment, lost souls scream in the agonies of hell fire. The Bible states clearly that the fires of hell burn forever and ever. The rich man lifted up his eyes from hell and begged Lazarus to bring a drop of water to cool his tongue. That story is no fairy tale, as many would have you believe. There is a hell to shun, but remember, there is a heaven to gain." He preached on and on, making every effort to scare the congregation into heaven with his awful descriptions of hell.

As we drove home, Mary asked me immediately what I thought of the sermon.

"God doesn't want us to love Him because we fear His punishment," I suggested, trying not to be too critical. "He wants us to be drawn to Him because of His love."

"You didn't believe a word Brother Wheeler said tonight, did you?" asked Sally.

"No, Sally, I can't agree with sermons showing everlasting punishing. The Bible reads clearly that those who choose to follow Satan instead of God face everlasting destruction. Even John 3:16 states that God wants to save us so we won't perish. To perish is to cease to exist. It seems clear to me."

Even as I talked, I sensed a weakness in my argument. My life didn't reveal what I preached. I belonged to a church that taught contrary to my testimony. I knew the fallacy of my friends' thinking, but they lived their belief. My life didn't back up my words.

I thanked them for taking me, then ran into the house to talk to my husband. Words poured from my troubled heart. "I must become a Seventh-day Adventist, Duane. The Nazarene evangelist preached about a hell that burns forever tonight. Sally and Mary consider me confused and deceived because I didn't believe him. How I want to live my faith so my life speaks truth to them!"

"You become a Seventh-day Adventist, and you say goodbye to me," Duane responded in a voice that scared me.

I could bear the frustration no longer. Tears flowed down my cheeks, but I immediately turned my face from Duane and walked to the kitchen to wash the dishes left in the sink. To my great surprise and joy, he joined me. He started rinsing and drying the dishes while he jokingly complained, "Those girls of yours are almost too much for me. I wanted to watch television, but they had me reading a book or holding a doll or playing a game all evening. I just got them to bed about thirty minutes ago."

"Don't call them mine," I said, blinking away the tears. "You have spoiled them just as much as I have."

"Thank You, Jesus, for softening his heart," I prayed

under my breath. I praised God for the good ending to a bad episode. Duane's rebellion against taking a stand on our newly found beliefs troubled me, but I knew he would change. The doctrines God had revealed to us were the answer for everyone. With every fiber of my being I desired to have my feet planted firmly on that truth so I could be powerful in sharing with my world. My passionate love for my husband gave me perfect faith that this would be done with him by my side.

6

A Second Call

"Please turn to page 141, 'All to Jesus, I Surrender,' for our closing hymn," Brother Haney said at the conclusion of his sermon the following Sunday morning.

"If there is anyone in this congregation who wants to commit his or her life to Jesus or who wants a special victory, come to the altar to pray as we sing. Let's all stand."

Duane, Lori, and I stood to our feet in our row near the front of the church. Duane held 2-year-old Tami in his arms, and we joined the congregation in singing the first verse.

"Go forward to declare your commitment to keep Sabbath." Immediately I stopped singing to hear words that traumatized my whole body. I looked to the front of the church, where it seemed as if I could see Jesus, standing in the midst of angels, pleading with me. It was like a repeat of the picture I had seen of Him in the choir loft when He had called me at 11 years of age.

Completely overcome, I lowered my head and hung onto the seat in front of me. My whole being cried out, "I can't! What will Duane do? What will everyone think?" The call and the sight of my Lord surrounded by angels were indelibly imprinted on my mind, and my heart burned with the most powerful manifestation of God's presence I had ever known.

It seemed like an eternity before the service ended. I carefully hid my feelings while Duane and I talked to fellow church members after the service. I didn't say a word on the drive home, but walked into the house and opened my Bible, looking for comfort. These words leaped before my eyes: "Blessed is the man that doeth this, and the son of man that layeth hold on it; that keepeth the Sabbath from polluting it, and keepeth his hand from doing any evil." Isaiah 56:2.

"God called us to Sabbath-keeping this morning," I cried out to Duane as he walked in the door. "He impressed me powerfully during Brother Haney's altar call. I saw Jesus and angels at the front of the church calling me to come forward to testify that I would keep Sabbath."

"You're getting carried away with this thing, Donna." The fire I had seen only two or three times before lighted my husband's eyes. His voice became ugly. "How could I keep my job if I kept Sabbath?"

"I don't know," I replied meekly, "but I know that the Sabbath commandment is still binding. If we love Jesus, we have to obey Him."

"You need to start thinking about something besides religion," Duane said in an angry voice. "We live in a

A Second Call 55

real world." He turned from me to walk to the bedroom to change clothes.

I wanted to say, "The Lord takes care of those who place Him first," but I knew Duane's mood held no room for argument. Immediately a plan began to unfold in my mind. "This week must be a time of prayer for me. When Jesus calls next Sunday, I'll respond, and my prayers will soften Duane to go forward with me. The Lord wouldn't call me without calling him. Next Sunday it will work out perfectly."

My desire to walk in perfect obedience to the truth included a need to have my husband beside me. I couldn't imagine becoming a Sabbath-keeper without him. By God's grace, I determined that prayer would result in both of us being totally committed, and on the following Sunday, we would both respond to God's call.

Even so, the following week was the most miserable time of my life. I prayed as earnestly as I knew how, but God seemed far away. Doubts plagued me. I asked myself several times, "What will we do a week from Saturday when we begin keeping Sabbath?" The question never received an answer. Blind trust assured me that everything would fall into place after our surrender.

Agony raged inside, but I acted happy and carefree on the outside. After the initial disagreement with Duane, all became peaceful between the two of us. He treated me sweetly, as though I had laid aside my intention to keep Sabbath. I chatted with friends at the basketball games and at Wednesday night Bible study. We spent our customary Saturday at the farm homes of our parents.

Sunday morning came. I resolved that on this day, as

the Lord called, I would commit myself to becoming a Seventh-day Adventist. I felt scared, but a week of torment made me anxious for the decision to be made so I could have peace. I refused to believe that Duane wouldn't join me.

There was no Saviour, no angels, no divine impression when Pastor Haney gave his usual call. Something inside forced me to walk up the aisle to the altar and kneel for a few minutes. The pastor immediately asked if others would like to join me for prayer. Several members came to the front.

"Father, send Duane," I silently pled over and over, but I knew my husband wasn't one of those at the altar. After just a few minutes, I stood to my feet and said to the congregation, "Studying the Bible has led me to the discovery that Saturday is the Sabbath. God is calling me to commit myself to keep that day from now on."

In my own strength I gave the promise, and now the weight of the world fell on my shoulders. Frantically, I looked for Duane and saw him standing near the front with tears streaming down his face. I realized they were not tears of sympathy, but tears of grief.

Church members came to the front to hug me and assure me of their support in whatever decision I made. Most of them knew about my Sabbath conviction, but loved me and were too kind to say anything negative. Finally, we were free to go home.

"Did you not feel called to make a Sabbath commitment?" I anxiously asked Duane as soon as we were in the car.

"I felt absolutely no call," he answered coldly.

"Duane, could I please call some Sabbath-keepers we might visit this afternoon?" I pled, feeling that I must have some support. I knew the woman who sold us *The Bible Story* books lived in Shattuck, so I thought we might visit her.

"I have no need to talk to anyone—I'm not a Sabbath-keeper. I'm going home."

He said nothing else, but I knew he was terribly upset. Both he and I barely touched the dinner that I placed on the table. After the meal, he went to the living room to read the Sunday paper, while I took the girls to their bedroom for naps. They slept, and I tried to read the Bible and pray.

"Where are You, God?" I called, but heaven's door seemed closed. "I thought You would manifest Yourself again today as You did last Sunday," I cried. "I didn't sense Your presence at all, and neither did Duane. Now I'm all alone as a Sabbath-keeper, and I don't know what to do."

I slipped back in time to my childhood commitment to keep Sunday holy. The same heavy load that had settled on my shoulders as I left the ballplayers that Sunday afternoon now rested on me in this new commitment to becoming a Sabbath-keeper. I sensed that my burden was the same kind that Jesus had felt at Calvary, but sadly, I felt no sorrow for His sacrifice. I thought only of myself and of the serious trouble my Sabbath-keeping was causing between Duane and me. In ten years of marriage, no conflict had come our way that was even close to the ocean-wide gulf separating us this afternoon.

For two hours I carried the burden, and then an idea

came. Immediately the load lifted slightly as I ran to the living room with a solution for all our problems. "Duane, what do you think about calling the pastor to visit us after the service tonight to give us counseling. We have a big problem, and we need help."

"An excellent idea," Duane answered, in a most pleasant voice. "Give him a call to see if he would be free to come."

I felt relieved and happy as I called the pastor to make the appointment. He readily agreed to the visit, and immediately after the evening service came to our house.

"You two are the brightest lights in our church," he began. "Donna, I think you've gotten discouraged because you look at church members instead of the Lord."

"No, that's not true, Pastor," I answered. "I'm unhappy with my church because I don't think we fully teach the Bible. For almost two years I've studied a correspondence course that shows verses proving the teaching of the Bible about the Sabbath, the state of the dead, and many other doctrines. The lessons have made me realize that my Methodist church teaches false doctrine."

"You believe Adventist doctrine from reading their Bible course," the pastor replied. "You need to understand that church denominations take verses out of context to prove their teaching. It's a way to confirm almost anything from the Bible."

"Oh, I don't think this study takes verses out of context." I immediately came to the defense of my new faith.

"Here's how you can know that I'm telling you the truth," the pastor continued. "The Catholic Church produces a Bible study, the Church of Christ offers one, and there are many others. Why don't you do yourself a favor by studying one of these, and then I think you'll see what I'm trying to tell you. However, before we go any further in this discussion, I want to ask you and Duane a personal question. Do you two study and pray together?" He looked first at me and then at Duane.

"No, Pastor," Duane answered. "I know we should, but we don't."

"Thank you for your honesty, Duane. Now I have a suggestion. You two need to read your Bibles and pray together every day. You have a wonderful home, with two darling little girls. I don't want anything to happen to it, and neither does the Lord. The very best insurance for happiness is to give God some time."

"You're right, Brother Haney," Duane answered. "We need to have devotions together every day. I'm willing to begin tonight."

"I'm certainly ready to have a worship time, too," I answered, overjoyed at Duane's response. "I think you've touched upon our real problem, Pastor. Maybe I'm trying to step out for the Lord, when I don't really have a good relationship with Him."

The words of our evangelistic pastor made perfect sense. I had attempted to step forward in a great move for the Lord, thinking I could bring Duane along with me, while we didn't even have devotions together. As we would study and pray, the Lord could easily lead us into Sabbath-keeping. The cross lifted from my shoulders, and happiness returned.

7

A Heavenly Touch

"Shall we start with our Bible reading tonight?" Duane asked as soon as the pastor left. "Yes," I agreed. "Bedtime is almost here, and I'd like to read at least one chapter."

Picking up our Bibles from the coffee table, we started in the book of Matthew. Duane read the first chapter about the genealogy of Jesus. When he finished, we made no comments, but I was first on my knees to pray. Anxiety grew intense as I whispered "Amen," eager to hear my beloved husband talk to God.

"Father, Donna and I should have been having devotions together our whole married life," he prayed in an amazingly natural manner. "We come to You tonight to begin anew, and we sincerely desire Your help. We truly want to serve You. Amen."

Our simple prayers brought great hope to my heart. "Surely God can work in our lives as we seek Him together," I thought. The following three nights became a harmonious, sweet experience. Every day I could think of nothing but the Bible studies my husband and I would share. Wednesday night before our devotions, Duane again confronted me, speaking in a tone that left no doubt of his desire. "What about this Saturday? Are you going to keep it like a Sabbath?"

With scarcely a thought, I gave him the answer he wanted to hear. "If God wants me to observe Sabbath, I trust He will reveal this to both of us as we study and pray together." His relief was obvious.

My conscience plagued me terribly as the end of the week neared. I had made an open commitment to keep Saturday holy. Suddenly a feeling of déjà vu swept over me. As a child I had made a promise to keep Sunday holy, but easily caved in to temptation in less than one hour. Now at age 28 I had made a pledge to keep the true Sabbath day holy. Again, as the cross came to rest on me, I rid myself of it in less than five hours. In both instances, I desired with all my heart to be obedient, but I didn't have the strength to stand for the Lord.

I soothed my wounded conscience with a hope that the Lord could draw Duane and me into Sabbath-keeping from our daily worship together. Then that dream began to fade as our time together hit many snags, finally turning into a formality that soon ended completely.

"God, show me Your way!" I pled, but my prayer seemed to go nowhere. I stopped studying Adventist literature, as my pastor suggested, and ordered Bible studies from the Catholic Church and the Church of Christ—and even material from the Unitarian church. None of the studies interested me enough to seriously learn about them; however, when I stopped reading Adventist literature to study other beliefs, I became confused. Many times I wondered if God had a real truth, or if, as so many thought, "It doesn't matter what you believe, as long as you believe and go to church."

Outwardly, our lives seemed perfect. Duane and I continued our work in the church as if nothing had ever happened. Church members accepted and loved us and seemed to have forgotten the words that I had spoken before them on that Sunday morning.

My spiritual life deteriorated; however, our home life became sweeter than ever on a cold day in December with an addition to our family. "We got our 'boy'!" Duane phoned to tell our parents, "and we named him Vonda Kay." We were momentarily disappointed that Vonda wasn't a boy, but we immediately loved our third blue-eyed, blonde-headed girl.

Duane got the position of school superintendent in Seiling in 1968 when Vonda was 18 months old. This moved us even closer to the farms where our parents lived, and we continued our weekly Saturday visits. We built a new home, in which we lived with our baby and Lori and Tami, who were now 6 and 9 years old. Duane enjoyed success in his work, and I continued my pastime of presenting memorized book reviews throughout the community.

For the next six years, we lived happily in Seiling, but our active life in the Methodist church could not extinguish a continuing faint desire in my heart to live according to the dictates of the Bible. After the initial confusion had passed following my effort to keep Sabbath, I had again in my mind embraced the doctrines of the Seventh-day Adventist church as truth. In my junior high

Sunday School class, I incorporated much Adventist teaching into my Methodist teachers' quarterly.

My spiritual growth, which seemed at a standstill in these years, was renewed when the church board asked me to speak for a Sunday night service in our church. I found a story about formality in worship, which I felt fit our lives, and with renewed hope, I typed the words for memorization.

A day or two before the date to do the program, I went outside to attempt prayer and to meditate on the words of my talk. Suddenly, the Holy Spirit touched me with a sense of love for Jesus. My languishing faith came to life, to believe for a glorious victory. The old dream filled my heart that the love of Jesus might also touch Duane, and our lives could become powerful for Him.

Since I knew Duane and I needed time with the Lord to learn to know Him, I planned a call at the close of the service. I determined to challenge the people to arise early each morning for one week to seek the Lord. If others would respond to this call, a miracle could take place in our church.

Amazingly, I continued to feel close to my Saviour as I stood before about twenty of our church members to make my presentation. As an introduction, I shared how God had called me from childhood to an intimate relationship with Himself, but I had only given Him a busy works program.

Then I quoted the story of Bron, a little English boy who had gone to church with his governess for the first time. He heard the minister tell about a brave and kind Man who had been nailed to a cross a long time ago, who feels a dreadful pain even now because His people aren't doing anything about it. In Bron's mind, the minister tells the story so the many people there will move immediately to right this injustice.

The service ends, and the people walk away as if they had not heard such terrible news—as if nothing remarkable had happened. As the boy and his governess leave, he is trembling. His governess leans down to whisper, "Bron, don't take it to heart—someone will think you're strange."

I made closing remarks: "God wants to set us free from the chains that bind us to the world—shackles which take away concern for our Saviour's death on Calvary. He can give us a living, vibrant faith such as Bron felt, if we will give Him some of our time. I feel His call to arise at 5:30 starting tomorrow morning to seek Him in Bible study and prayer. I challenge you to join me at the altar to make this commitment for at least one week. Let's put God to the test to see what He can do for us."

It thrilled me to hear Gene Crane say immediately, "Friends, I don't know about you, but I feel the Holy Spirit tugging at my heart. I'm going to join Donna." As he came forward, his wife Sally and six others followed, making a total of nine people willing to make this simple promise. I couldn't believe the Lord could work through me in such a powerful way.

Unfortunately, Duane wasn't one of the nine. As we returned home, his stony silence loudly proclaimed his disapproval. Sorrow kept me awake for hours, but I arose for devotions at 5:30 the next morning.

"Good morning," I said in my cheeriest voice as Duane

came to breakfast an hour and a half later. He gave me a cold, icy stare, turned his head away while he ate, then left for work without a word.

A few minutes later Sally came to tell me exciting news. "Your presentation and call last night thrilled Gene and me. We got up at the scheduled time and had a wonderful hour with the Lord."

"Duane is very angry about the service," I confessed immediately, and then burst into tears as I told her my difficulty. "To keep peace in my home, I probably won't be able to keep my commitment past this week. I feel awful, but what can I do?"

"Oh, you poor darling," Sally comforted me, hugging me tightly. "You do what you have to do. Gene and I will pray for you, and the Lord will see you through."

As the week progressed, I continued to keep my appointment with the Lord. Duane's silence and scowls showed his exasperation. On Thursday he said contemptuously, "You wake me every morning when you get out of bed at this ungodly hour. Just what can it possibly accomplish?"

"I'm sorry I made the promise," I said submissively. "I agreed to do this for one week, and I must keep my word. But I will stop after Sunday morning." After four days of living with his displeasure, I felt I could bear it no longer.

The experience broke my heart. God had revealed His presence to me so beautifully that I had felt certain Duane would respond positively. Again, my husband had refused to cooperate with my plan for his spiritual life. In tears and sorrow, I cried out to God, "Why didn't Duane come to the altar? Why does he fight me? You've got to touch him, or we're never going to be able to do a work for You, Jesus."

My mind couldn't imagine a religious work that didn't include my husband. But something new had happened in this episode. God's power touched me in a way that moved others. Duane's love was vital to me, but this experience brought a taste of what heaven could give me. With a whetted appetite, I knew that somehow I must seek for more.

8

Memorization

Looking into the faces of our Methodist congregation, I quoted with pathos the words of Jeremiah: "Before I formed thee in the belly, I knew thee, and before thou camest forth out of the womb, I sanctified thee, and ordained thee a prophet to the nations." Jeremiah 1:5.

Success attended my every word. My thoughts ran rampant. This is the fulfillment of my dream of a new life of service to God. Jesus desires to make Duane and me His prophets to uplift truth in a dark world. My heart overflowed with happiness at the thought.

As eloquently as I could speak, I presented the verse that would be the theme of our work: "Obey My voice, and I will be your God, and ye shall be My people." Jeremiah 7:23. I wanted those words to convey the message that the Ten Commandment law is still in effect and that the Sabbath day of the fourth commandment must be kept holy. How I thanked God that both Duane and I recognized this truth. I turned my eyes in his direction, hoping to see his positive response, but unlike the rapt attention of others in the group, his head was down.

I prayed a quick prayer that the message of Jeremiah was touching his heart. I knew that if he could realize on this night the new ability the Lord had given me to memorize and quote the Word, he would recognize God's hand over our future. His public school career would end with a call to the Kingdom—a bidding not only to make us Seventh-day Adventists but also leaders to warn people to keep God's commandments or face destruction.

Earlier, Lori, Tami, and I had waited in the family room, while Duane and Vonda had gone to the station to put gas in the car. I decided to tell my 12- and 15-year-old daughters of the experience that had my heart overflowing with joy. To gain their full attention, I stood to my feet, then spoke passionately. "After 39 years of coming to Jesus and falling away, surrendering anew, then backsliding again, I've found the solution that will keep me living for Him forever! The answer is so simple that it boggles my brain—it's the memorized Word of God. With the Bible in my mind, possibilities for me to be powerful for the Lord have never appeared brighter."

"I know you've always dreamed you could do great things for God, Mom. I can't imagine how memorizing could have brought a new discovery." Lori's expression betrayed her skepticism. She and Tami sat on the divan dressed in jeans and shirts to attend their Methodist Youth Fellowship meeting.

"Believe me, it has happened, and it's for real!" I exclaimed, backing up so they could get the full impact of my words. "You remember that in a talk last January, only eight months ago, I called church members to com-

Memorization 71

mit to rise early for devotions. The people responded, but your dad didn't like it when I left his warm side to rise early for time with the Lord, so I backed down. Immediately, my religious zeal dimmed, but Jesus mercifully touched my heart only three months later with the idea to use the Bible for my memorized presentations."

"Do you mean that your program tonight is going to be just Bible?" Tami asked doubtfully.

"Yes! Just as I've always taken exact words of authors to write book reviews, the Lord has sent the idea to practice the same style with books of the Bible. I felt impressed to go to Jeremiah, so I selected verses from this book, then carried my typed sheets to the golf course, where I could walk and memorize. With this plan it seemed that the Lord had given me a new opportunity to live for Him, so I knelt to pray for forgiveness of all past disobedience and then for a revelation of truth as I learned His Word.

"God answered that prayer as I spent about an hour each day repeating verses to place them in my mind. My relationship with Jesus grew more real with every verse. I sensed that I was on the verge of a tremendous move from heaven. The fire in my heart that had been slowed after I failed to follow through on my commitment to rise early in January blazed again. The heavenly Father literally stepped down from heaven in His Word to feed my hungry soul and save me in spite of myself."

"Sounds like God has really touched you," Lori said.

"Yes, I truly feel His hand upon me, and it thrills me to think about the future. I know the Lord loves me, and with all my heart I plan to pursue His will. Satan has held me a helpless captive for years, while deliverance has been as close as my Bible."

"I wish Lori and I didn't have to go to the youth meeting so we could hear your program," Tami lamented.

"If tonight marks a new beginning for you, we should be there," Lori added.

"I wish you could be in the sanctuary for my talk, but you must attend youth group because your sponsors expect you. Besides, I'll tell you all about it tomorrow. I truly think I'll have exciting news, because I began a no-sweets fast four weeks ago to call down the power of God on my presentation. The fast, coupled with the Word I've memorized, makes me know He's with me tonight."

"You've kept your fast a secret," Lori observed. "I haven't noticed that you hadn't been eating desserts."

"And neither have I," Tami said.

"Fasting displeases your dad, so I've been careful about my eating habits when he's home. I'm praying with all my heart that through my presentation, God will send a spiritual call to him, because any plan God has for me must include your dad."

Tami stood to her feet. "It's time for us to go. I hear Dad sounding the car horn."

Happy at the positive response of my daughters, I gathered my Bible and papers, and we walked to the car for the short drive to church.

"Vonda, I'll send you to the front when your mom has said enough tonight, and you can tell her it's time to sit down." Duane gave me a knowing wink.

Memorization 73

"OK, Daddy," Vonda answered. "I'll do it, but I want you to go with me."

Laughing at the thought of such a crazy action, I glanced at my husband, who after twenty years of married life still treated me like his girlfriend. His support was vital to me, and I could hardly wait for his reaction to my Bible presentation—a talk I truly believed would bring a turning point in our lives. My speech calling for conviction to rise early had angered him, but after a recent seven-minute talk for our worship service, made along with three laymen, he remarked, "You bested three guys in the pulpit this morning!"

Now, in the closing minutes, I introduced the last section. "The example we find in the book of Jeremiah speaks to us of our prospective future. The prophet preached this message for forty years. King Josiah listened and led the people in revival, but the following three kings refused Jeremiah's counsel. Finally, under King Zedekiah, they were taken captive to Babylon, exactly as the words read: "Judah shall be carried away captive all of it . . . Give glory to the Lord your God before He cause darkness, and before your feet stumble upon the dark mountains, and, while ye look for light, He turn it into the shadow of death, and make it gross darkness." Jeremiah 13:19, 16.

"We need to listen to these words," I told my audience. "The Jews heard but failed to heed. They were taken into captivity for seventy years. God calls us to simply obey His Ten Commandment law and in that way give glory to Him. Otherwise, our fate will be the same as that of the Jews."

Again I recited verses that pointed me to the Seventh-day Adventist church in the role of a modern prophet Jeremiah. I had no desire to reveal this to my Methodist brethren on this night. Instead, I longed to be a member of the Adventist church, which I knew fully taught the truths of Jeremiah, and then to present this message to all the world.

Memorization had written God's law in my heart, placing me on an upward path that would ultimately lead me to that fulfillment. I felt lifted to the skies as I closed with beautiful verses of promise. "For those who will allow it, God says,

" I will put My law in their inward parts . . . and will be their God and they shall be My people . . . and cause the Branch of righteousness to grow up unto David . . . and this is the name wherewith she shall be called, the Lord our righteousness." Jeremiah 31:33, 33:15, 16.

Prayer ended my thirty-minute presentation; then the blessing of heaven enveloped my whole body as the small congregation came forward to congratulate me.

Taking both my hands, Allie Strecker spoke glowing words: "I didn't know you could memorize Scripture so fluently. I've been in this church for years, and your talk tonight was one of the best I've ever heard."

"You spoke the Word plainly tonight," Woody Wood said, while Gladys stood by his side shaking her head in agreement. "You placed the verses of Jeremiah in just the right sequence to make a powerful message."

Within a few minutes, each person in attendance had come forward to give compliments. Every word fed my confidence. My fasting and prayers had moved the arm of God. Tonight was the first step in a mighty work. As

Memorization 75

the last member walked away, my thoughts suddenly turned to my husband, my coworker in the Lord's vineyard. I couldn't wait to hear his approval of my new speaking material. My eyes scanned the sanctuary. I couldn't find him. Where was he? Frantically, I looked at the people leaving. He and Vonda were not among them. What had happened? Why did he not look at me during the presentation? Where had he gone?

9

Growth

"Where did Duane go?" Norman asked as he and Jackie drove me home from the church. "I was busy talking and didn't notice," I answered, speaking casually so they wouldn't realize the fear in my heart.

They dropped me off, and I dashed into the house. Duane sat in his favorite chair in the family room. A dark thundercloud seemed to hover over his head. "Duane, what is it? Why did you leave early? Why did you come home?" I leaned over him in my anxiety to have his reassurance that everything was fine.

An ugly look distorted my handsome husband's face as he stood to his feet to speak in a defiant voice: "I'm telling you right now that I'm not going to live with a woman who is a preacher!"

He said no more, and I knew nothing to say to him. He stalked to our bedroom while I stood in the family room gathering my thoughts and crying to God, "What has gone wrong? Why can't he see that the two of us could present truth and be instrumental in leading people back to You just like Jeremiah? Why is he angry, when everyone thought I did so well?"

I kept my face dry, but cried buckets of tears inside as I joined my husband in bed. He stayed far over on his side. His indifference broke my heart, but I realized God had touched me mightily. In the past, I would have put my arms around him and said the words he wanted to hear, "Duane, I'm sorry I acted like a preacher. I won't do it anymore."

No way would I say those words. It had been thrilling to present the Jeremiah book review for my church. I had sensed God's power on my presentation, and I couldn't wait to compile another program from another book of the Bible. No way would I give up what had just been given to me.

Neither would I give up this guy who lay like a stone beside me. I could have both—God and Duane. I determined that he would soon feel God's touch through the sweetest wife in the world. He wouldn't be able to resist me, and thus I could draw him to Jesus. Our great work could begin!

My heart was lifted heavenward to pray, "Now Your hand must be placed on my husband. He's disturbed because he sensed Your power in me. He has sat on the throne of my life for years, Jesus. It has been bad for him and bad for me, but now You can lead me onward to full commitment and use my life to win him. Duane has always been such a good leader that if he were totally committed to You, he and I could be powerful in winning souls. Please make that dream come true soon."

Growth 79

With the success I now felt in my spiritual life, I determined to do everything possible to make that prayer come true. Duane must be won to the Lord and to Sabbathkeeping. When he came home in the evening, I made certain I was always attractively dressed, with my hair freshly combed. I baked homemade bread and broiled T-bone steak. His interests were the subject of my every conversation, while religion remained on the shelf. I practiced every feminine wile to regain his affection. Nothing worked.

He often spoke to me in cutting words that hurt immeasurably. "Why do you have to be so different from everybody? What do you think you accomplish with your piety?"

"I love the Lord, but I don't consider myself better than anyone." I spoke in a gentle tone, trying to appease his anger.

Immediately after the Sunday night presentation, invitations came to present my Jeremiah program at both the Friends church and the Christian church in Seiling. I happily wrote the dates on my calendar. The local civic women's club, of which I was a member, also scheduled me to do a lesson. Since I wanted to write a new Bible presentation from the New Testament, I decided to use the book of John for the program. While memorizing this gospel, the Lord brought me even closer to Himself than He had with the book of Jeremiah. Within days a message enlightened my mind: "But as many as received Him, to them gave He power to become the sons of God." John 1:12.

I recognized that hiding the Word of God in my heart from both John and Jeremiah enabled the Lord to transform me into His image. It seemed to require no effort—the Word washed away my worldliness, while in its place came a spiritual blessing that brought double satisfaction.

For instance, my morning routine included watching the "Dinah" television show. I now felt impressed that the program wasted my time. A keen sense of heaven's approval came when I stopped watching it. A second step took place when the Lord awakened me early one morning for a walk and talk with Him before breakfast. The beautiful morning, along with the special sense of the nearness of God in His great outdoors, made this activity a habit from that day forward.

The Lord also led me to fast. Even as I sensed a special connection with heaven on my no-dessert fast before my Jeremiah presentation, fasting meals now wrote a special covenant between my Saviour and me. I would omit meals—and perhaps this spiritual discipline would reveal to God the intensity of my desire that He save my husband. During the mealtime, I usually took a walk to pray and memorize Scripture.

At first, I fasted various meals, always setting a time when Duane was away from home. Invariably, he discovered my pursuit and shouted his resentment: "Why can't you be a normal Christian instead of a Pharisee?" I solved that problem when I made Wednesday noon a fast every week—the day he ate at the Lion's Club.

After more than twenty years of sweet married life, the growing trouble between us was difficult for me to accept. However, for the first time in my life, I had a hold on God that I refused to surrender. I sensed Duane's jealousy of my relationship with my heavenly Father.

Growth 81

That understanding enabled me to be kind to him even as he remained cold to me.

Then late one night when he and I were alone in the family room, a miraculous softening occurred. I attempted to bridge the wall between us as I looked up from the divan where I sat putting a hem in Lori's skirt. "Duane, I gained the most marvelous insight from the book of John. As we feed on God's Word, He actually changes our desires to transform us into sons of God."

His impassive face suddenly softened. I boldly plunged ahead, "I know your concern about me becoming a Seventh-day Adventist. I've removed Sabbath-keeping from my mind, while God changes me day after day through the power of His Word. When He wants me to keep Sabbath, He will lead in that step." My words were true. I so wanted to keep Sabbath, but even with all my spiritual growth, this step overwhelmed me. I truly trusted God to lead me into His perfect will.

My simple words melted my husband's heart, and he stood with a sweet expression on his face. Sensing acceptance, I immediately walked to him and threw my arms around him. He pulled me close. "I treat you mean, and I'm sorry," he said. "I hate what's happening to us, but an unexplainable feeling possesses me. This morning I prayed for a sign about Adventism. The school day passed with nothing special taking place. When it came time for the buses to leave this evening, Pastor Bonn came to talk to me before he got on his bus.

"He said, 'I know Donna shows great interest in the Seventh-day Adventist church. I studied Adventist doctrine several years ago. Their teaching made sense, and I almost joined their church. However, I continued to search and realized they base their beliefs on the law, which makes their teaching legalistic. Since God today leads His people by His Spirit, we don't need the law. I hope you can help your wife to think clearly about their message.'

"He got on the bus, but I knew as I walked back into my office that the Lord had answered my prayer through Pastor Bonn's conversation. The Seventh-day Adventist church is not for us."

His words both thrilled and disappointed me. I felt joy to know that he cared about our relationship, because his indifference had made me think that he felt no concern. The seemingly negative message about Adventism saddened me, but I sensed it came because he couldn't bear truth, so I agreed with him as I reveled in the joy of his strong arms around me again. I looked up to say, "God answered your prayer, darling."

A few days later on my morning walk, an insight flooded my mind. "Pastor Bonn possesses a character above reproach, yet at funerals he preaches everyone into heaven. In his church he never takes a firm stand against sin. Duane has talked to me many times about his strength as a man, yet his weakness as a leader of people."

Overwhelmed, I knelt immediately to thank God. "How powerfully You work in ways past our understanding! You gave Duane a perfect sign on Monday. Show him this insight today, that he may know the Seventh-day Adventist church *is* for us."

After months of trouble, our life together took on the aura of a honeymoon. We were both best friends and sweethearts and could hardly find enough time to be together. He often came home to eat dinner with me, as he did on a Tuesday morning only a few days later when he called from school to say, "I'll be home in a few minutes for dinner."

I happily cooked black-eyed peas frozen from our garden and served them with homemade bread. I greeted him at the door with a hug and a kiss and an apology for the simple lunch. "You didn't give me time to cook anything special."

He sat down at the bar and said our blessing. With the first bite, he gave a compliment. "These peas taste better than anything they're having in the school cafeteria. Besides, I need pleasant company. Teachers have been in my office all morning with grievances. One of the board members came to see me because parents are up in arms about our hair code. My job gets tougher every day. For my health's sake, I need to look for less stressful work."

A light bulb snapped on in my mind. "Let me fast and pray for you to find more satisfactory employment. I'll eat no goodies—cake, pie, cookies, or candy—until the heavenly Father places you in an easier job. Fasting brings power with God. He might give you new work soon. What do you think?"

"I hate for you to deny yourself, but I surely would feel relieved to walk away from this situation. It's totally up to you." Duane buttered another piece of bread and took another helping of peas.

With happiness flooding my heart, I repeated my commitment: "From this day I eat no goodies until we see heaven move us from this place."

We finished eating, and then went to the family room, where he sat in his recliner. I climbed onto his lap and placed my head on his shoulder. "God made this body part to be my pillow," I remarked.

"Your head rests there every night and part of every day. That's the reason for the indentation in my shoulder," he teased.

We talked a few minutes, then he went back to school. I cleaned the kitchen with a singing heart. My praise became even louder on Thursday night when we went to Enid to a Prophecy Crusade. Norman and Jackie had heard the advertisement on television and invited us to go with them. I said nothing, but the title made me think it could be an Adventist series, and I was right. We heard Dan Simpson, a Seventh-day Adventist evangelist, present the United States in Bible prophecy from Revelation 13. The four of us sat spellbound, listening to a message proving that our great nation would ultimately speak like a dragon.

On the ride home, Duane made an astounding observation, "That preacher spoke sound doctrine. I wonder why there was such a small crowd."

In my thoughts, I answered him, "Only a few people attended, because truth isn't popular!" I dared not say a word, but his remarks made me realize anew that my husband believed the doctrine of the Adventist church. I dreamed fantastic dreams of our work for God as we rode the eighty miles home, and the others discussed the school and community affairs.

Then came Christmas and a confrontation with Duane that ruined our sweet communion. About a month earlier, I had realized that Christmas fell on Wednesday this year. How I wanted to forget my Wednesday fast, but I knew that I couldn't lay aside this small sacrifice without a similar falling back in my relationship with God. The thought of not eating at our big family gathering on Christmas day scared me. What would the family think? What would Duane think? I prayed about it daily.

The day arrived, and we joined Duane's extended family and my parents (who were often included) at his grandmother's home for the celebration. When it was time to eat, I helped Vonda fill her plate. Family members lined up, there was much talking, and I felt relieved to realize that no one would notice I wasn't eating.

But there was one who saw. Duane stood last in line to get his food. He came into the kitchen where I sat with the girls to ask, "Aren't you eating?"

Very quietly, I replied, "No."

He violently threw his filled plate across the cabinet. Luckily, it stopped at the back, leaving the food intact. "You have to be the most stupid human being in the world."

He spoke quietly, but both his facial expression and his voice conveyed his disgust. He said not another word, but left his food on the cabinet and joined the others in the dining room.

I thanked God that no one but our girls knew about our fuss. In a few minutes I took my place with the family and talked nonchalantly to various ones, while my heart cried out to God, "I did it for You, Father. Why did You let it ruin my relationship with Duane?"

Finally the day passed and we returned home. I walked into our house with a heavy heart as Duane again treated me with cool silence. Our several weeks of good communication gave me great hope, so I clung to faith that the Lord would soften his heart again. Duane's displeasure hurt immeasurably, but I knew that his fight against God brought his ugliness. He saw the handwriting on the wall. Continued memorization of God's Word would make me a Seventh-day Adventist.

After years of dreaming of a work for God, I eagerly anticipated becoming a Sabbath-keeper to fulfill the dream. No power on earth, not even my husband, could stop my spiritual growth. Yet I continued to believe that my faith and prayers would soon bring Duane to the same experience, in spite of his present annoyance.

During this time of spiritual growth and trouble in my home, the Lord brought two special friends who gave me support. Mary Ellen King, my next-door neighbor, always lent a sympathizing ear. Jackie Louthan and I shared on the telephone and often went to the church to pray. I talked Adventist doctrine to both of these women and took them through the *New Life* studies. Both seemed to believe every teaching.

Jackie thrilled me with this observation after she learned about the state of the dead and the destruction of the wicked: "Duane teaches these truths in his Sunday School class. I think he believes like a Seventh-day Adventist as much as you do." Relief flooded my heart. No matter how ugly he acted, God was at work in my husband's life. His total surrender, I was convinced, was only a matter of time.

Twenty months had passed since my Jeremiah presentation. In the meantime, I had learned and presented five other books of the Bible, not only in my town of Seiling, but in several surrounding towns. Memorization of the Word lifted me closer to God daily, but love for my husband prevented an important step. I couldn't surrender to the Sabbath.

In April, Dan Simpson held an evangelistic crusade in Okeene, a town forty miles from Seiling. Because they had heard of our interest in Adventism, he and the pastor came to Jackie's house to visit and invite us to the meetings. My conscience plagued me as he spoke to me personally before he left: "Donna, when are you going to make a decision to keep Sabbath?"

"I don't know." His direct question made me uncomfortable, but I couldn't give him a positive answer.

"You're the leader of some of these Christians in Seiling. When you decide fully for Christ, many of them might follow you." His words touched my heart. I knew this giant step must be taken.

As the week progressed, I sensed that Elder Simpson and other Okeene church members must be praying for me. It seemed time for me to make a decision to keep the Sabbath. This was a critical weekend for the school—the band follies were scheduled for Friday night, and the junior/senior banquet and prom were to begin at 6:00 on Saturday night. Although I knew the superintendent's wife should be at both activities, I determined that from this Saturday I would keep Sabbath, preventing my attendance at both festivities.

With strong determination, I approached Duane about an hour before the Friday evening program. My courage immediately wavered as I looked at his unfeeling face. He treated me so coldly these days that I could hardly stand to tell him my plan, but I summoned all my nerve. "I'm going to keep Sabbath. I can't go with you to the band follies."

With a scowl on his face as if to say, "I hate you," he marched to the bedroom, closed the door, and dressed to go to the program. I sat on the divan feeling lost and alone as I watched him and the three girls leave. His anger drove away the sweet presence of the Lord, whose Sabbath I planned to observe.

"I'm going to do it this time!" I told myself all evening. I took a walk, prayed, and studied. Troubled feelings ruined my blessing, but I felt that after I kept this Sabbath, future ones would be happier and easier to observe.

When Duane and the girls returned less than two hours later, I sat on the divan waiting for them. He coldly informed me, "You can sleep there tonight. I don't want you in my room." With that, he went to our bedroom and shut the door. I talked to the girls for a few minutes, and then we went to bed.

All night I tried to pray, but my prayers seemed to hit the ceiling and bounce back in my face. "Jesus, I'm keeping Your Sabbath. Where are You? You promised a blessing if we keep Your day holy. Sometimes You're so close to me. Where are You tonight when I need You?"

Duane left early on Saturday morning to go to the farm. I felt grave concern about what he would tell our two sets of parents about my absence, but determined to worry about them later. On this, my first Sabbath, I decided to seek the Lord at home instead of going to church. Church was twenty miles away, and I felt too overwhelmed to leave the house.

All day I tried to study and pray. I talked to the girls about my beliefs and my hope for us as a family. But never had I felt so weak. Constantly thoughts ran through my mind, "What did everyone think when I didn't show up at the follies last night? What will the teachers think when I'm not at Duane's side at the banquet tonight? How sad for Duane to be alone at the prom! Will he decide he won't tolerate a Sabbath-keeping wife?"

He returned early to get ready for the evening. The doubts that burdened my heart brought impulsive words, "Can you go without me again tonight?"

His answer came quickly and curtly, "You bet I can!"

It was too much. My resolve melted. "I'm going with you." I hated myself for failing, but I couldn't bear another minute of misery.

I donned my prettiest dress and went with him to the school's most gala affair of the year. I felt happy to be by the side of my successful man, yet sorrow filled my heart. It seemed that no matter how much I read or prayed or tried, I couldn't take the stand for my Lord to actually keep Sabbath. I felt like a lost cause.

The evening was wonderful. Duane's anger melted away, and he treated me as his own special girl. We ate at the head table, listened to the program the young people presented, then watched them dance until midnight. All the time I prayed to my Lord, "Jesus, You understand how I feel. You know how weak I am. I so want to keep Sabbath, but I can't do it without Duane by my side. Please bring him to commitment so we can be about our work for Your Kingdom."

10

Surrender

Duane recognized my growing commitment when I arose early every morning for devotions. He sensed my deepening relationship with the Lord when he saw the pages of Bible texts to memorize that I kept with me constantly. He noticed the more spiritual comments I made at Wednesday night Bible study. My failure to stand firm and keep the Sabbath the night of the banquet momentarily sweetened his personality, but he knew the score mounted against him day after day. For a few days, he treated me with kindness and affection. Soon, however, this sweet time ended, and he turned cold. Again, my pain returned.

A summer vacation to Colorado with our neighbors, Bob and Mary Ellen and their son Mike, drove me to a decision between my husband and my God. All the way from Oklahoma, I attempted to talk to him but had no success. After arriving in Durango, we boarded a train for the four-hour trip to Silverton, an old mining town. Since I continued to hope that this trip could bring about our reconciliation, I sought to penetrate his cool exterior. I moved from my seat on the train to sit beside him, then made my plea.

"Let's make this train ride a new beginning for us," I suggested. He ignored me, moved to sit by Bob, and began a conversation with him.

Not willing to give up, I tried again to make conversation on the trip down the mountain. Again I moved to his side. "Duane, doesn't this remind you of the train ride we took to Washington, D.C., with the Dill City seniors in 1962?" He didn't look at me or answer. Instead, he got up and walked to the other side of the car.

Throughout the trip, he teased the girls and Mike. I sensed that his joking with Bob and Mary Ellen made the trip enjoyable for them, but he treated me as if I weren't one of the group. Embarrassment and sadness triggered the prayer: "Enough is enough! I'm waiting on this man no longer. When we get home, Father, I promise to give it all to You."

We returned home, but the same old doubts plagued me. I truly wanted to become a Seventh-day Adventist, but I thought of my husband, my family, my friends, and all the complications involved. "How can I keep Sabbath?" I asked my heavenly Father. Miraculously, I opened my Bible a few days later to read the answer: "Then will I sprinkle clean water upon you, and ye shall be clean from all your filthiness, and from all your idols, will I cleanse you. A new heart also will I give you, and a new spirit will I put within you: and I will take away the stony heart out of your flesh, and I will give you an heart of flesh. And I will put My Spirit within you, and cause you to walk in My statutes, and ye shall keep My judgments, and do them." Ezekiel 36:25-27.

Surrender 93

A new insight came to me. According to these verses, God could make me do His will. I prayed an earnest prayer: "Because I'm afraid Duane will leave me, I can't keep Sabbath, Father. I've tried over and over, and I've failed every time." Then I continued with my first positive Sabbath-keeping prayer: "I'm willing to be made willing. Put Your Spirit within me and cause me to keep Sabbath."

Amazingly, God answered my prayer that week when the Seventh-day Adventist Church in Okeene made another effort to reach interested persons in Seiling. When they called, Jackie invited them to come to her house. Four church members and the pastor came the following two Wednesday afternoons to pray and share with us. Jackie, Mary Ellen, and I, plus a few other friends, listened to their inspiring testimonies.

The young pastor, Larry Zuchowsky, told about his life. "I was raised in this church, but not until five years ago did I learn to know the Lord. Conversion to Jesus has changed my life. Not only do I want people to understand the doctrine of my church; more than that, I desire to lead them to Him."

"I've been an Adventist all my life, but Jesus became my best friend only three months ago," Eva Voth, the leader of the group, said as she gave her testimony. "Now my faith no longer consists of dead works. I love and serve a living Saviour."

Their stories made an impact on me. Both the pastor and Eva seemed to love Jesus as I had imagined every Adventist did. I went home from both meetings greatly encouraged. A feeling of freedom overwhelmed me by the Thursday following the second meeting as I thought, "The Word in my heart for the last two years has performed miracles to make me an overcomer. I walk in harmony with the Lord on every issue except keeping His holy day. He can easily continue His work and make me a Sabbath-keeper if I will just trust Him." Fear died, and trust in Jesus filled my heart. I knew a bigger miracle had occurred.

That evening I called Eva, who had given her witness at the prayer group. "Please send someone to talk to me Friday evening. I think I'm going to join the Adventist church this Saturday, but I feel the need to share with a church member before I take that step."

Friday evening, soon after Duane and the girls had left for the football game, I was pleasantly surprised to see the pastor and Eva at my door. It had not occurred to me that my telephone call would bring the leader of the church. We sat together in the living room, and they listened attentively as I told of my years of struggle, beginning with my attendance at Emmanuel Missionary College twenty years before. They heard my whole story, often asking questions to spur me on. We talked for about two hours, and then they rose to go. I sensed their happiness in the decision I had made.

As soon as they were gone, I walked to the golf course where I had sought the Lord many times. The full moon and twinkling stars created a beautiful atmosphere for my victory prayer. Peace that passes understanding filled my heart with love for the Saviour. I praised Him for not giving up on me, as I lifted my face toward heaven to cry, "Your Word has written Your law in my heart for over two years. Finally, I have victory over the last area—Sabbath-keeping. All I had to do was allow You to make me willing.

"Now that I'm wholly Yours, precious Saviour, You can answer my prayers for my dear Duane." Tears streamed down my cheeks as I thought of my husband. "I know he'll be saved soon, and he and I can work together to win our world. People will listen to our testimony when we practice what we preach. Hasten the day! We've wasted too much time.

"Oh! But You must be with me in the days ahead, Father. This is a giant step for me because of Duane, our girls, and the rest of our families. My role as the wife of the school superintendent magnifies the problem. These people love me, but they have no understanding of Your truth. As You carry me perfectly through the days ahead, many of my friends and family will join in this great work."

I basked in glory as long as I dared, then returned to the house to await Duane and the girls. They soon came, and we went to bed. No one realized the great happiness hidden in my heart.

Sabbath morning before getting out of bed, I said to Duane, "I think I'm going to join the church today." "I think" sounded weak, but he knew I meant it. Without responding, he quickly arose, dressed, and left. His distress made no impact on me. I sensed a new confidence in the power of the Lord.

I explained my plans to the girls, then drove to Okeene to the Seventh-day Adventist Church. The pastor and Eva thought I should go to this big church to make my commitment; however, I knew that after today I would attend the small church at Canton only twenty miles away. I sat quietly in a Sabbath School class, then listened to Pastor Larry preach a stirring sermon about the Christian race based on Romans 12. Every word touched my heart on this day when I fully felt my involvement in that race.

We stood to sing the closing hymn. I waited expectantly for the pastor to give an invitation, but he gave none. At the beginning of the last verse, I slipped from my place to walk to the front of the church to stand beside him. "Here I am to become a member of God's true family," I whispered softly.

The song ended, and the pastor spoke again, "It gives me great joy to introduce Donna Nicholas to you. She comes from the Methodist church in Seiling to become a member of the Seventh-day Adventist church. Please give her a warm welcome." Then turning to me, he asked, "Would you like to say a few words?"

I stepped to the podium. "Today marks the end of years of struggle for me. The Lord has brought me to surrender and I'm happy to follow Him in perfect obedience." It seemed so simple, yet I knew that I had made the most important decision of my life.

After the service, I stayed for the fellowship dinner. Many members came to welcome me and get acquainted. Then the pastor took me aside to share and pray. I felt totally drained as I confessed to him, "Ecstasy filled my mind with words of praise after you left last night, but today I have nothing to say."

"After your high, it's only natural for you to feel

empty," he comforted me. "Obviously, the Lord has led you to take this important step. Be assured that He will soon lift your feelings."

He prayed for me, and I left to drive home with the question repeating itself in my mind, "What will happen now?" I still had confidence, but it seemed strange to me that I felt so void of feeling. I intended to go straight to my house, but the Holy Spirit impressed me to tell my Methodist pastor about my commitment. Obediently, I drove to his house.

Our Methodist pastor and his wife, a young couple whom we loved dearly, had been with us only a few months. I had never shared my beliefs with them; however, in our small town it was common knowledge that the superintendent's wife was pro-Adventist, and he was radically opposed.

"I expected to hear this," the pastor commented after hearing my witness. He made no effort to reason with me but simply said, "I'm sorry to lose you, but I know you must follow your convictions."

"I feel really sorry for you," his wife, Cindy, said sympathetically. "This won't be easy." I knew she spoke of my situation with Duane.

"Thank you, Cindy. I appreciate both of you, and I've loved working with you in the church. Even though I'm becoming a Seventh-day Adventist, I hope to continue attending church with Duane and the girls."

The kindness and understanding of Pastor Don and Cindy brightened my spirits. Making my witness known for the first time drove away a little of the emptiness, and the presence of the Lord became more real. I hurried home to share with my girls. They gathered about to listen to the day's happenings. "Pastor Larry didn't give a call, but I knew I was going to make my commitment. The devil and all his angels couldn't stop me today. And now that it's behind me, I can't believe that such a giant step became so easy. I have a deep feeling of peace and confidence. I know I did the right thing."

"Yes, you did, Mom," Lori said. "You believe the Sabbath, so you had to become a Sabbath-keeper."

"What about Daddy? What do you think he will do now?" Vonda's face showed a worried frown.

"Honey, I have more confidence in your dad becoming a Seventh-day Adventist now than ever. The Lord couldn't answer my prayers for him to be fully committed when I wasn't fully dedicated myself. One hundred percent of me belongs to the Lord now. I expect miracles!"

"For Dad to become a Sabbath-keeper would be the biggest miracle I can think of." Tami stretched her arms wide to signify size. "I surely hope he does, but regardless, I'm glad you made your decision."

"Thank you, honey. All three of you have supported me through these two years of struggle. I appreciate your positive attitudes. It would have been far more difficult if you had opposed me like your dad has." Suddenly, I realized a new spirit within me. "Girls, do you know something incredible? Sharing with Pastor Don and Cindy increased my faith. Now telling you gives me even more confidence. Let's run next door to tell Mary Ellen the news."

By nightfall I felt like Martin Luther who had nailed

his 95 Theses on the door at Wittenberg. Sharing my faith removed the emptiness and filled me with the blessed assurance that I now walked in perfect obedience with the Lord. My life lay in His hands. I happily anticipated an exciting future. The fact that Duane didn't come home by bedtime in no way dimmed my ardor.

The girls and I went to church the next morning, even though Duane wasn't home to go with us. There, another test awaited me. I knew I must inform my junior high Sunday School class of my decision. I had taught this age group throughout the eight years we had lived in Seiling. I dreaded telling them of my resignation.

As closing time neared, I breathed a prayer, then made my confession. "Yesterday I joined the Seventh-day Adventist church. Bible studies for the past several years have proven to me that I must keep the seventh day holy. I no longer feel spiritually secure in the Methodist church; therefore, I will be going to church on Sabbath. However, I will not leave you young people. I plan to continue coming to church here with my family."

It was easier than I could have dreamed. The youth assured me that they loved me and wanted me, no matter what church I attended. The dismissal bell rang. I stood amazed to discover that the word spread like wildfire throughout the church. Friends crowded around me as I went to the choir room to put on my robe.

"Donna, we don't want you to leave us to attend another church," Mildred mourned. "We can't do without you."

"Oh, I'll keep going to church here," I assured her.

"Yes, but it won't be the same," Ada commented.

I gave no answer. We marched to the sanctuary to take our places in the choir loft, but my heart sang through the whole worship service. I sensed a perfect peace with God, along with the acceptance of my Methodist pastor and friends. Questions vaguely pulled at the corners of my mind—Why have I not seen Duane? Why did he come to teach his Sunday School class, then leave before the worship hour? I drove the doubts away with happy thoughts of the grand work he and I could now do for the Lord. All these precious people in the Methodist church could be brought into the truth through our influence. Now that I'm one hundred percent the Lord's property, He can put His wonderful plan into motion to accomplish great things for His Kingdom!

11

Confrontation

"You must be pretty proud of yourself." Duane's blazing eyes and cutting words revealed his feelings of abhorrence. "You have divided our family. After going to the Methodist church all your life, you now belong to the Advents. Mark this in your mind, Donna—I won't live with a woman who belongs to a cult. You will leave!"

His demeanor scared me. My self-assured husband, who criticized anyone not living an orderly life, seemed out of control. It was Tuesday morning, and I stood at the kitchen sink washing breakfast dishes when he stormed into the room. It was the first time I had seen him since he had left the house on Saturday morning. Endeavoring to keep my composure and talk quietly, I dried my hands, then turned to face him. "Just because I'm a member of a different church doesn't mean we can't live together."

"Oh yes, it does," he promptly replied. "You no longer love me. You love that church and those people. I refuse to put up with it."

"I do love you, darling." Praying that God would touch him, I suddenly saw my husband as a weak man threatened by a no-longer submissive wife. My fear subsided, and I looked at him with compassion. "I've always loved you, and I always will. Now that I've put God first, I love you even more."

"You haven't put God first," he quickly retorted. "You've placed a church first. The Bible clearly says that a man is the head of his house. Since you listen to the Advents, I'm no longer the head in my home."

How I longed to throw my arms around him as he raved on and on. He spoke the ugliest words he could think of, but I never took my eyes from his face. I prayed over and over, "Touch him, Father! Touch him, Father!" My own confidence in standing firm before one who had brought me to my knees many times amazed me. I also recognized my own responsibility for our current problem—losing his position of first place in my heart after twenty-two years had turned him into a jealous husband.

With a final stipulation, "Pack up and move in with the Advents!" he returned to work. I was relieved to see him go. As much as I loved him, I didn't like his almost-violent behavior. I turned back to the sink to finish my task with a prayer of thanksgiving on my lips. God had seen me through my first big hurdle in the faith. I comforted myself that Duane's words were only a whim. Surely, he didn't really want me to move.

As the days passed, he repeated his words daily. His behavior remained mean and intolerant. I hated hearing the door open, knowing he had returned home, because he always came straight to me to ask cruelly, "Why

Confrontation 103

haven't you moved out?" I became concerned that I must go away.

The girls gathered about me, and Lori asked the question that was on all our minds. "Where can you go, Mom? The grandparents support Dad, so you can't stay with them."

"I don't know. Your dad scares me because he's acting crazy. I know I need to leave, but where do I go?"

"It makes Dad angry because your faith is right and his belief is wrong," Tami said knowingly.

"Yes, you analyzed the situation correctly. The whole world may disagree, but this is right, and here I stand! Since your dad knows this, we must be patient with him. The Lord can still use me to turn him into a Sabbathkeeper. But in the meantime, I don't know what to do."

No answers came as we pondered the dilemma. Then came a turning point on a day when I lost my temper. Because I recognized my husband's weakness, I more easily kept my feelings under control. While he raved at me, I always looked lovingly in his eyes and prayed, "Touch him, Father." But I lost control one day when he stormed into the house, fuming, "Get out of here today! Go live with the Advents you love so dearly!"

In response to his enraged behavior, I screamed back at him, "Quit yelling at me! You know my belief is right! You're just as much an Adventist as I am."

"Don't call me an Adventist!" he shouted, and then slapped me across the mouth. Immediately my lip puffed big and red, and Duane's anger melted away. He gently led me to the bathroom, where he wet a washcloth and placed it on my mouth. "Never have I been so glad to be hurt," I thought to myself, as I gloried in the joy of his attention. Then he turned from me, fell on his knees, and cried like a baby.

I put my arms around him, "Don't cry, darling. It's OK."

"I'm sorry I hurt you. I couldn't control myself."

He stood, and I threw my arms around him, but he coldly pushed me away. "Don't think I love you, because I don't. I'm just sorry I hurt you."

That momentary victory answered my prayer. I now knew Duane really didn't want me to leave. He truly loved me, but now that I had placed the Lord first, he felt hurt and fought against me. With renewed courage, I prayed for my dear man.

Because our lives were so intertwined with our parents' lives, our trouble affected them profoundly. Facing their displeasure bothered me immensely. Since my faith didn't conform to their standard, both families sympathized with Duane. My parents came to talk on a day when Duane and the girls were at school. Since my daddy had a quiet, very tolerant disposition, my mother thought his disapproval would make an impact on me. As they came in, she said, "Your dad has something to say to you."

"What is it, Daddy?" I asked, praying silently that I could make peace with my beloved parents.

"Honey, I don't know what you're thinking about in joining this church. Your mom and I don't want your home wrecked, and that's what's going to happen." Daddy spoke in a voice choked with emotion while the

Confrontation 105

heartache written on both their faces was almost more than I could bear.

Praying for wisdom, I said, "Daddy, you respect other people's beliefs. You know that I believe the fourth commandment is still in effect. I must be a Seventh-day Adventist to have peace with God."

Mom interrupted before my daddy could respond. "That's what we can't understand—why you think you must go to church on Saturday. Look at our family—your grandparents, your aunts and uncles, your brother and sisters—they all go to church on Sunday. Your actions condemn their belief. Honey, these Adventists have led you astray. Forget what they tell you and use common sense. God doesn't want a broken home, and these strange ideas forecast the end of your home."

"It doesn't matter what my family believes; I have to follow the insight God has given me. Perhaps when I share with my family why the Sabbath is important, many of them will accept it, too. And Mom and Daddy, you don't need to worry about Duane leaving me. He loves me just as I love him. Our marriage can weather this storm and come out better than ever. Besides, Duane believes the Sabbath and other doctrines of the Adventist church. Right now, he refuses to practice them."

"Of course, he can't be an Adventist," my mother responded. "He would lose his job if he refused to work on Saturday. It's very sad, too, that you won't be able to attend many school activities with him now because you're keeping this day. It's foolishness, honey. God wants peace in our lives, not confusion."

We talked for about an hour. I did my best to defend

the faith, but my parents didn't comprehend a word. They could only think about the fact that my belief jeopardized my home; therefore, in their opinion, the situation must be corrected. I also sensed that my new commitment shook the pride that both sets of parents felt in our success in the community.

Their sorrow filled my life with unhappiness, but then I found words of comfort: "If ye be reproached for the name of Christ, happy are ye; for the spirit of glory and of God resteth upon you: on their part He is evil spoken of, but on your part He is glorified." 1 Peter 4:14.

I could hardly bear the pain my family troubles caused my parents as well as Duane's parents and our girls, yet the blessed assurance filled my heart that God was by my side and that I should praise Him for the privilege of suffering reproach for His name. The trouble proved I walked in truth.

I never dreamed Duane would stop my attendance at the Methodist church, but the next Sunday morning as I started to get dressed, he stated in a tone that dismissed all argument, "You will no longer attend my church. Your church can be sufficient for you now."

A sinking feeling overcame me, but a voice inside told me to be quiet. I watched my husband and girls drive away, then sat on the divan to cry bitterly. I could hardly stand for my family to go to church without me. Then a verse I had learned came to my thoughts: "And He shall bring forth thy righteousness as the light, and thy judgment as the noonday." Psalm 37:6.

With that verse running through my mind, I walked to the golf course to seek the Lord. "Father, my heart breaks to be here while my husband and children and my friends meet in my old church. You spoke to me to leave the situation alone. I must commit it to You, but please hurry to bring forth my righteousness as the light. Then my husband and children will join me in worship instead of going to a separate church."

Suddenly the Holy Spirit descended upon me to heal my hurt and change my thinking. I immediately realized I should be thankful to stay home. Two mornings every week in church services would take much time from my schedule. With a grateful heart, I returned to my house to prepare dinner.

At first Duane insisted that I must leave, but I stayed, and he took no action. Therefore, I didn't pay much attention when he made his next demand: "I refuse to support an Advent. Get yourself a job."

"Oh, you know I love to be home. It would be hard on the girls for me to work away from home."

"You should have thought of that before you joined that church. Since I'm no longer the head of the house, you can make your own living." He continued telling me this day after day, but I ignored it. One morning he came from school, placed the car keys in my hand, and literally pushed me out the door, speaking in no uncertain words, "Find yourself a job today." I had no desire to find a job, but in the hope of keeping peace in the family, I set out to look for one. Fifteen years had passed since I last taught school. With the fall term well underway, I had no hope of finding a teaching position.

I drove to Woodward, a larger town thirty-five miles away, and parked on Main Street, wondering what to do.

108 SWEET MADNESS

All my confidence vanished. I felt lost and alone. Even the heavenly Father seemed far away as I prayed, "What do I do? I don't know how to get a job."

I stepped out of the car and walked aimlessly up and down the street. I looked at stores but had no courage to enter. Then I saw a dress store that looked inviting, so I walked inside. The clerk finished waiting on a customer, then turned to me, "Could I help you?"

"Do you need extra workers?" I timidly asked.

"No, I'm sorry, we have no openings now," she answered.

I covered two blocks in both directions, then returned to the car feeling more troubled than ever. "I've been out of the job market too long," I said to the Lord. "I don't know where to look, and I don't know how to ask. Tell me what to do. Remember, You promised: 'Trust in the Lord, and do good; so shalt thou dwell in the land, and verily thou shalt be fed.'" Psalm 37:3.

Discouragement destroyed any faith I might have had in the prayer I had just prayed. I thought to myself, "This is too much! I'm going home to tell Duane that I can't find a job." The thought of his response added anxiety to my troubled mind. I started the car and drove west. About four blocks down the street, I suddenly looked up to see the answer to my prayer on a sign in front of me—"State Employment Agency." I couldn't believe my eyes. I parked and went inside.

The woman at the counter looked at me expectantly. "Are you looking for work?"

"Yes," I answered confidently, smiling. "I'm a former teacher with a degree in business education and speech, and I want to return to the work world. Are there any jobs available?"

"You came at a perfect time," the woman answered. "We have two offices hiring for secretarial positions. Complete this application, and we'll send you for an interview."

I wrote the needed information and went for two interviews. One company offered me a job immediately, and the other said they would call in two days. My depression lifted. All the way home I praised my wonderful God for His perfect care of me. Duane seemed a little happier when I gave him the report. I told him I would accept one of the positions, and when the second company called, I went to work for them because of their shorter workday. My work hours plus the fifty-minute drive required me to leave home before my family left for school and to return home after them in the evening. The girls adjusted quickly. They prepared supper, we ate as soon as I got home, then we did the housework. Duane remained cool, but he gave me no more ultimatums.

I enjoyed being a secretary, a position I had held my first two years of marriage. I still believed, however, that Duane would soon become a Seventh-day Adventist, and I could then resign my job. In my mind this work simply passed time until we could take up the more important task of winning souls. When the winter months passed and there was no change, I determined to renew my certificate so I could teach school. I attended the summer session to work on an elementary certificate at the university in Weatherford; then the Seiling Board of Education hired me to replace the fourth-grade teacher who was taking a year's leave of absence.

Since Duane had been instrumental in hiring me, I assumed his attitude would become more tolerant. But he remained aloof, both at home and in the school. I made friends with all the teachers, but it seemed impossible to gain my own mate's love. However, the hope burned brightly in my heart that we would soon be a united family in the truth and that he and I could fulfill God's ultimate plan. His cold treatment could not quench my dream.

Duane came home with exciting news at the end of the school year. "I've been hired to be the director of the Educational Service Center in Cushing, in eastern Oklahoma. This means goodbye to the headaches of running a public school."

The promotion brought joy to his heart. How I wanted to tell him that I believed God had answered my prayer and fasting by giving him this great new job, but I dared not mention anything spiritual in his presence. With a thankful heart, I went to my tree on the golf course.

"Father, thank You for giving Duane a great new job in response to my no-goodies fast. Now I'm going to make another covenant with You. I want to end my Wednesday noon fast to omit meals as You lead, but I'm going to renew my no cake, pie, cookies, or candy fast to enable You to move an Everest-sized mountain. I'll not eat these desserts until You make Duane and our three girls Seventh-day Adventists."

12

The First Sheaf

Hope that our move to Cushing would soften Duane toward my faith soon met disappointment. He persuaded the superintendent of schools to hire me to teach fourth grade, but he continued to treat me with cool indifference.

Perhaps my active life in the church fed his bitterness. Soon after our move, I discovered six Adventist families in Cushing. I became friends with the Sweets, an older couple, and we worked together to encourage these people to meet with us on Sabbath in a local rented building. Since I became a leader in this group, I spent much more time in church work than when I lived in Seiling.

On the Sabbath of our official organization, the Lord's blessing overshadowed Duane's disapproval. In addition to three men from the conference office and our own people, several Adventists came from the surrounding area to make a group of thirty-five people. To my great surprise, Lori and Tami entered the room when the service began. My joy knew no bounds. How I prayed the service would impress these girls!

After the fellowship dinner, I noticed Tom Good, the evangelist sent by the conference to help us, talking to Lori. I pretended not to listen as he encouraged her in our faith. "When are you going to allow us to baptize you? A girl like you doesn't belong in a public university. You should attend our college in Keene."

Lori laughed but gave no response. I felt a momentary disappointment that she had no interest, but excitement banished negative thoughts. My mind overflowed with dreams of great success for the Cushing church, and I planned to devote every free minute to helping make it prosper. This church brought the possibility of fulfillment of my desire to exalt the truth I now embraced. Some of the Adventists in Cushing were spasmodic in attendance at the churches where they now belonged, but I clung to the thought that God would enable me to bring them back to their first love, plus win many unbelievers.

Monday morning I went to school as usual. As lunchtime neared, I felt a strange impression that I should fast. Since I felt hungry and knew no reason not to eat, I pushed the impression away and enjoyed a good dinner.

About 6:00 that evening Lori called from Stillwater, where she was a sophomore at Oklahoma State University. I nonchalantly answered the phone to hear her ask, "What do you think about me going to Southwestern Adventist College next fall?"

My heart leaped into my throat. Had I heard her correctly? "It would be great! Would you like to go there?"

"Yes, I would."

"Lori, do you want to become a Seventh-day

Adventist?" I asked hesitantly, fearing a negative response.

"Yes, I do, Mother!" I almost dropped the phone as my 20-year-old spoke these long-awaited words.

"I can't believe this is happening. You've never said a word."

"I've thought about it for a long time, Mom. The Bible shows that Sabbath is God's holy day. I must be in the same position you were in three years ago when you wanted peace with God but had to become a Sabbathkeeper to find that satisfaction. I'm no longer happy in the Methodist church. Jesus calls me to take my stand for His truth."

"What an answer to prayer, honey!" Tears of joy streamed down my face.

"Congratulations to you for being the first new member of our Cushing church. You must call Pastor Tom."

"I'll call him tonight." Then hesitantly, she asked, "What do you think Dad will say? I'm afraid to tell him."

"Your decision will be a blow, but the Lord can use your commitment to save him," I consoled her. "God will pave the way for you to talk to him."

We said goodbye, and I fell to my knees to praise a wonderful heavenly Father, who had listened to my constant prayers for a husband while He had worked mightily to save a daughter. I realized that the impression to fast had come for her sake; therefore, I fasted and prayed all day Tuesday and again on Thursday. God's great goodness had performed an unexpected, unbelievable miracle. His blessings lifted me above earthly concerns as I taught my fourth graders and worked at home through the remainder of the week.

Lori told her dad her plans on Friday night, then reported to me. "Dad said, 'If that's what you want, go for it. I assure you that the Adventist church is a cult, so don't expect any more financial help from me.' I know it hurts Dad for me to transfer from the state university to our church college, and I'm sorry about that, but I don't mind being on my own financially. The Lord promises to take care of me."

"Yes, God will take care of you just as He has provided for me. I gave up my role as housewife when I became an Adventist, but I don't mind working. It's worth any price to walk with our God in His truth."

My heart burst with pride on Sabbath morning when Lori took her stand at the close of our church service. Since I hadn't been rebaptized when I became an Adventist, I asked Pastor Tom to baptize me along with Lori. The service took place in the Stillwater church on the following Sabbath afternoon.

"This was the most thrilling day of my life! Now I'm a full-fledged member of the remnant church." Lori's face reflected her happiness as she drove us home after the baptismal service.

"I feel that same excitement, honey. Baptism renews my enthusiasm for the work. How I pray your dad will soon unite with me to proclaim this truth from the highest mountain for all the world to hear. He's such a good leader. Together we could do a wonderful work. I desperately want to be more zealous in saving souls, but with your father's opposition and my need to teach school, it seems I have little time."

"If your prayers for Dad are as powerful as your prayers for me, he'll join us soon. Then you can work full time for the Lord." Lori spoke encouraging words as she turned into our driveway.

Another surprise came when she called the following week. "I became a vegetarian. Do you know of any food I can eat besides Stripples and Grillers that I buy at the store?"

"I'll have to think about it." My daughter's decision stunned me, but I quickly recovered composure. "What an Adventist you are! I haven't even tried to stop eating meat, and you change a few days after baptism. Since you've never liked animal products, vegetarianism will be easy for you."

"Yes, Mom, you forced me to drink milk. I'll never drink another drop."

"Forgive my ignorance, honey. The meat and dairy industries have pounded the value of eating their products into my head since childhood. The church teaches that vegetarianism is the better way, but fear of your dad's irritation has prevented me from taking that step. Enough foolishness! Regardless of his feelings, I'll join you in this venture. From now on, I'll eat no meat."

"Great! Come up with some ideas for us," Lori begged. "The girls in my apartment expect me to starve if I eat no animal food. I can live on potatoes, but I guess I should have a few other foods."

After my promise to search for recipes, we said goodbye. I became a vegetarian at my next meal. Most of the time various legumes replaced the meat in my diet, and I never missed it. My new way of cooking became fun as I experimented with patties and vegetarian recipes for myself and Lori. Duane didn't say a word, although he had to notice that I no longer ate anything from the meat platter that always sat on our table.

God provided amazingly for Lori at Southwestern Adventist College. She found a good job, enrolled in a full class load, and loved her new life as a vegetarian Seventh-day Adventist. When she came home during a college break, she teased Tami, "How sad that you live in the dark!"

I gloried in her confidence, but Tami retorted in sibling fashion, "I'm as good as you."

Lori's buoyant faith made a strong impression on Vonda, who confided in me a few days later, "I believe like you and Lori. Pray that I can make a decision to go to your church."

My youngest daughter's words delighted me. "Of course I'll pray, and I'll also fast for you. God can make this step easy if you depend fully upon Him."

Our conversation took place on Tuesday. For the next three days Vonda's sad little face told me that she struggled as I had when I tried to become a Sabbathkeeper without relying on God's power.

Finally, on Friday, she confessed, "I can't become an Adventist now. I'm afraid to tell Daddy."

"That's OK, honey," I assured her. "Don't give up. Continue to seek the Lord in Bible study and prayer. Since you're Daddy's special girl, the one he loves to tease

The First Sheaf 117

and take places, you could be most influential in leading him to unite with us in faith."

Her face brightened. "I hope so. I'd love for all of our family to be Seventh-day Adventists."

"That's the day I dream about. You and Tami will make your commitment, then with four in the fold, Duane will realize he has lost the battle. With his surrender, the war ends, and the Lord wins!"

At the end of only two years in Cushing, Duane came home from work to announce his promotion to the Oklahoma State Department of Education as director of the Educational Service Centers. I congratulated him for this nice promotion, but under my breath I praised the Lord for another wonderful answer to my no-goodies fast (which now included making my whole family Seventh-day Adventists). This fast, begun in Seiling to get Duane a new job, I was convinced had brought about his better job in Cushing. Now the Lord had given him an even higher position in Oklahoma City. In spite of the fact that I hated leaving the fledgling Cushing church, I looked forward to a new location, perhaps just the place where Duane's heart would be melted.

Because of my obsession with the salvation of my husband, the Lord constantly surprised me with special blessings. Before our move I attended an all-day church meeting in Oklahoma City. The principal of Parkview Adventist School learned I was a teacher, interviewed me, and hired me that day to teach at the church school the next school year.

I returned home to happily announce to Duane and the girls, "I have a job teaching fifth- and sixth-grade classes next year at the Adventist school in Oklahoma City. My salary is a few dollars more than I made this year in Cushing."

"I'm sorry you got yourself a job. My new boss promised to find you a teaching position in the area." Duane spoke with disappointment.

"How kind of him!" I awakened from bliss to realize that my blessing had hurt my husband's pride.

"You don't need me, Donna. Why don't you go it alone?" Duane's words sent a shiver down my spine.

"Yes, I do need you. I love you, darling. If it weren't for the opportunity to teach in a church school, I'd love to take the job your boss could give me." I spoke gently, hoping to heal his wounded spirit. I longed to throw my arms around him to show him how much I loved him, but for months he had allowed no such demonstration.

He left me alone with my thoughts. The idea of teaching and fostering faith in the lives of young people thrilled me, but my husband felt threatened. His cool demeanor never warmed these days—now it might turn icy. This frightened me.

13
The Next Sheaves

Duane and I bought a lovely home in Piedmont, a suburb of Oklahoma City, where we could easily drive to our new jobs. Tami moved to the dorm at Oklahoma State University to begin college life, and Vonda enrolled in the eighth grade in the Piedmont schools. Only Lori made no changes as she started her junior year at Southwestern Adventist College in Keene.

Even as I had discovered that many Adventists had little zeal for the work, so now I was disappointed to learn that the students at Parkview Adventist School lived surprisingly like the young people I had worked with in my Methodist church. I had visualized our schools as filled with students dedicated to Jesus. Along with my goal to win my family, I resolved to bring revival to this school.

I spoke to my twenty-five fifth and sixth graders almost immediately. "Young people, God raised up John the Baptist to prepare the way for Christ's first advent. Today, God has brought the Seventh-day Adventist Church into being to prepare the way for Jesus' second coming. Since we seem to lack the fervor displayed by John the Baptist, could it be we lack the power of the Holy Spirit?"

Immediately Terri Voth, one of my fifth-grade girls, raised her hand to ask, "How would the Holy Spirit give us power?"

"The Holy Spirit gives love for Jesus. 'The love of God is shed abroad in our hearts by the Holy Spirit which is given unto us' [Romans 5:5]. Love for Jesus would bring revival, because we would be filled with the desire to live and work for Him. I want that love, don't you, Terri?"

"Yes, I do."

"The disciples sensed such burning love for Jesus that they took the gospel to the whole world in ten years. We must pray that the Lord will give us that same kind of love so we can impact the world with our message. Would you young people like to set aside 1:00 every afternoon in this classroom to pray for the power of the Holy Spirit?"

An immediate chorus of "Yes!" encouraged me to continue. "Let's also make this a time to pray for family members. I want you to pray that my husband, Duane, and my daughters, Tami and Vonda, will become converted Seventh-day Adventists. Now if you'll give me the names of your unsaved loved ones, we'll have prayer." The students made their requests, then took turns praying down each row. Faith rose in my heart when I heard many of them pray for my family.

After teaching in public schools where I kept quiet about God, I reveled in the privilege of promoting faith

The Next Sheaves 121

in a classroom; however, within weeks a discipline problem that had plagued me in the public schools now surfaced also in my church-school classroom, threatening my spiritual influence. Students didn't obey me as they should. The principal attributed the trouble to my sympathetic nature that started each morning with a sweet spirit, but as the day passed and the students became unruly, turned into a loud voice that tried to bring order. I prayed about it daily and had many good days, but it seemed an ongoing battle that defied victory.

Soon I returned to memorization of large portions of Scripture, presenting the story of Joseph at a Monday morning assembly before the whole student body and teachers. This time learning verses was made easier as I used first-letter helps—a mnemonic device I had read about in a book from the school library. I typed verses from the account in Genesis, then wrote the first letter of each word on cards to carry with me, to memorize in my free time.

Again my presentation brought compliments, but most of all, the verses encouraged my faith. I recognized myself in Joseph, a spoiled son who lost his sweet life with his father, but after years of slavery and prison was exalted to be vice-president of Egypt.

For several weeks I claimed promises of Joseph in prayer. "Father, You plan to reward my faith just as You rewarded Joseph's trust, but we won't have to wait thirteen years. Our slavery/prison time ends soon with Duane's return. We'll begin our work to feed Your starving people, starting with revival in this school."

The following summer brought me great hope for the

salvation of my middle daughter. Lori, who had just completed her junior year at Southwestern, found a job for Tami working in the stick-horse factory at Keene. The Oklahoma Conference required me to take twelve hours of Bible to be a certified teacher in Adventist schools, so Tami and I moved to Keene to live with Lori and her roommate, Laura, in their rented mobile home. Tami went to work immediately while I enrolled in summer classes. Vonda divided her time among her daddy, other relatives, and us.

Having Tami with me in this Adventist atmosphere strengthened my faith to keep her there. Early each morning found me at a lovely place near the campus for my personal prayer time. There I claimed the promise of Jacob for Tami, also for Vonda and Duane, "I will not let Thee go, except Thou bless me." Genesis 32:26.

The first day of my "Life of Christ" class, a young woman who sat behind me shared her personal problem. "My future seems uncertain. I desperately need to know the Lord's will for my life."

I knew immediately that the Lord had given me a prayer partner. "I have three family members whom I urgently want the Lord to save. Let's go to the bench beside the administration building to pray for our special requests as soon as class ends every day."

She agreed, and that day the two of us knelt beside the bench to pray. The group grew daily as we invited others. It seemed every student I talked to had an illness, a troubled home, an unsaved loved one, or some other need. By the end of the first week on campus, a group of eight met every morning to share and pray together.

The Next Sheaves 123

I requested prayer for Tami not only from this prayer group, but from almost everyone I talked to for any length of time. A special blessing came one evening after study time in the library. On my way home I passed two young men standing on the sidewalk near the college entrance. Their friendly faces impressed me to stop and talk. From their broken English, I understood that their home was in Brazil.

"My 19-year-old daughter works at the stick-horse factory. Would you pray with me that God will impress her to stay here to attend Southwestern?"

They happily agreed to my request, and we knelt together on the sidewalk. I prayed first, then my new friends prayed in Portuguese. I walked home beside my Saviour with a new faith that their other-tongue prayers had moved His arm.

Disappointment awaited me at the end of the summer classes as I prepared to return home. Tami handed me a big box to take to my car. "I'll need these at Oklahoma State University." I prayed with tear-filled eyes as I placed the box in my trunk, "Father, she's only a sophomore. You can bring her here next year."

The following week, the three girls and I shopped for new clothes in a store near home. I overheard Tami say to Lori, "I won't need many new clothes since my old ones will be new to the students at Southwestern."

"Tami, are you going to Keene this fall?" My heart pounded in disbelief and happiness.

"Yes, Mom, I guess I am. I hated to tell you sooner because I haven't been sure I wanted to make the change.

"How awesome!" I hugged her close. "I asked everybody I met in Keene to pray for you to stay, but you showed no interest, so I gave up for this year. My wonderful God surprised me again!"

Vonda now stepped up to me. "Mom, if Tami goes to Keene, I'll go with you to Parkview."

"Vonda! You, too! Oh, how wonderful!" I turned from Tami to put my arms around my youngest daughter. "The Lord has answered my prayers exceedingly abundantly above all that I could ask or think! I've prayed for you this summer, too, but with almost no faith. I must think you're still a baby. You're another surprise from my mighty God!"

Our interest in clothes faded, and we immediately returned home. Even though both girls dreaded telling their dad about their plans, each found a time to talk to him. Tami reported that he accepted her decision but told her, as he had told Lori, that she would receive no more financial help from him. His words to Vonda brought her great concern. "Daddy said that if I attend Parkview, he's going to leave. He won't leave if I go to school with you, will he, Mom?"

"I'm not at all concerned that your dad will leave. He makes threats, but he has no more desire to leave us than we have for him to go." Duane's indifference couldn't touch my high spirits. It seemed the Lord had opened heaven to pour out a blessing so big I couldn't contain it. I had done very little study with the girls, making me know their decisions had been brought about through the power of prayer. I determined to pray more earnestly to bring about the greater miracle of their dad on his knees.

Life returned to normal a few days later when Lori

and Tami left for Keene. I went to the living room to begin polishing the television. Duane came from the bedroom to speak with a note of finality: "I'm listing this house in Sunday's paper. When it sells, I'm leaving. I want no part of a family who are all in Advent schools." He turned and walked into the garage.

A shiver ran down my spine. I caught hold of the television for support. "He's really disturbed," I said to myself. "He didn't show his true feelings to the girls." Then a happy thought came. It took weeks to sell our house in Cushing. The market is still slow. I lifted my eyes to heaven. "You won't allow our house to sell, will You, Father?"

The Lord had sent me so many affirmative answers that I had forgotten that He sometimes says, "No!" I would have trouble remembering this in the days ahead as well. A young couple came the following Wednesday and bought our home. As if in a dream, I went with Duane to meet them at the bank to sign papers.

Duane now pointed out the next step. "I'll give you sixty thousand dollars to buy a house for yourself. You must look immediately, because we have to be out of this house by the middle of the month."

I refused to look. Duane and I had lived together twenty-seven years. It couldn't be possible that he really wanted out of our relationship.

Three weeks passed. He looked at me from across the breakfast table. "What do you plan to do?"

"I'm waiting on you." I took a bite of toast while I gazed out the window.

"Donna, you can keep your head in the sand and refuse

to believe that I'm leaving, but I *am* leaving you! You'd best find a home for yourself, or you'll be sitting in the street." With that said, my husband got up from his chair and went to work.

I looked, then selected a lovely home on an acreage at the edge of Edmond. It cost more than my allotted money, but it was a perfect place for Duane and me. When he saw it, he spoke sharply, "Open your ears and hear me! I'm not moving with you. I refuse to tell you again or look at another house that costs more than the money I'm giving you."

My body went numb. I had refused to believe our house would sell. Yet it did! I hadn't thought Duane would leave. Yet his threats no longer sounded like idle words. Then a comforting thought renewed my faith. "Father, You must be allowing Duane to leave so You can save him. You can touch him more easily if he's away from us."

With a new hope, I went to a real estate agent. She found me a lovely three-bedroom brick house in a nice neighborhood in Edmond only seven miles from my school. Again, God led so miraculously that I felt my situation was His perfect will.

About four weeks later the movers set the last piece of furniture in my neat little home. Duane supervised every step, then turned to me. "The house seems to be in good condition. I'm going."

I desperately wanted to ask him to stay, but he had ignored all pleading, so I resisted the temptation to say more. I walked with him to his pickup and looked at him with my heart in my eyes. "Goodbye, Duane."

The Next Sheaves

"Goodbye." He backed out of the driveway and drove off into the night.

Tears blinded my eyes. I turned to walk into my new home. An uninvited guest joined me, making his presence known by an awful pain that lodged in my chest. I knelt beside my bed to cry to my heavenly Father, "I didn't think it would ever come to this, but I trust Your plan. My first little sheep, Lori, resides in the fold. The next two, Tami and Vonda, now attend Adventist schools and will soon join us. Now I'm going to move Your arm to save their dad. Tonight I'm 'weeping, bearing precious seed' [Psalm 126:6], but doubtless I will come again with rejoicing, bringing all four sheaves with me."

14

The Valley

Perhaps the Lord sent the good news of Tami's baptism soon after Duane left to strengthen me for a trial that lay ahead. Vonda and I journeyed to Keene to witness the momentous event. The influence of Bible studies given to her by her boss in the administration department, and the inspiration of a class on the life of Christ, led her to commitment. Happiness overflowed within me as my middle daughter participated in the ordinance that bound her to the family of God.

After the service we returned to Lori's rented mobile home, where she opened her refrigerator door to show me her milk. "Mom, this milk comes from soybeans. Laura and I made a New Year's resolution to become total vegetarians. We constantly experiment with recipes. Except for cooking, I haven't eaten animal products since I've been an Adventist. Now I'm not going to use any animal products at all."

"I'm proud of you, Lori. You've become my conscience in the health message." I placed my arm around my oldest daughter. "God commands us to bring our diet back to the original plan, so I have no excuse to continue eating dairy products. It's late for a New Year's resolution, but I shall become a vegan, too. Thank you, honey, for leading the way."

"What about me, Mom? Do I have to give up drinking cow's milk?" Vonda looked at me questioningly.

"No, I won't force my lifestyle on you, but I hope you listen to Jesus to surrender everything He asks of you."

"Don't mention total vegetarian to me," Tami piped up. "I'm taking the giant step of giving up meat. Jesus leads one step at a time."

In my naivete, I didn't dream the day would come when I would hear the news Vonda brought soon after our return from Keene. She had spent the night with her dad and then reported to me, "Daddy has a new friend who lives near him. You should see her—she's so pretty, with blue eyes and beautiful brown hair. She's much younger than Daddy and has a daughter exactly my age."

"How did you meet this woman?" We were on our way home from school. I kept my eyes on the road and gripped the wheel, steeling myself for the words she might speak.

"She planted flowers in Daddy's flower beds." Vonda smiled to herself as if remembering the pleasant evening. "She showered attention on me and told me that her daughter and I would get along well together."

"Oh God, this can't be happening!" I screamed in silent prayer. "Duane has never loved anyone but me, and I have never loved anyone but him. He's just lonely. You've got to protect him from all these man-hungry females out there."

"Do you think your dad likes her?" I felt I had to have her opinion even if it meant bad news.

"Daddy just likes her for a friend. I don't think it's anything to worry about." Vonda spoke reassuringly, sensing my concern.

My daughter labeled the friendship innocent, but fear drove me to my special place of prayer. Soon after our move, I had discovered that the beautiful Church of Christ college campus across the street from our housing addition made a great place for my morning walks. I went to an area west of the buildings where an open field sloped down to a small pond. Near the pond, I found a tree trunk sprawling across the ground. As I knelt on the trunk to pray, I gave it a name: my "Storm the Gates of Heaven Altar." There I prayed for all my requests, then stormed heaven's gates for my runaway husband.

Now with this situation before me, I earnestly prayed at that altar every day, claiming promises I had memorized. "Father, this time You've given me a mountain. The Anakims are there, and the cities are great and fenced, but if You'll be with me, I'll be able to drive them out! 'Now therefore give me this mountain!' [Joshua 14:12.] Oh, Father, You've allowed a woman to come into the life of my husband. You must not let this relationship blossom into love. Level this mountain, Lord, just as you did for Caleb."

It seemed my whole world was caving in as the next day the principal called me to the office to talk to me about my classroom control. He happened to pass by my classroom at the end of the day to hear me scream at the children, "Get in your seats and shut your mouths!"

He became very serious with me. "I think your problems at home are being carried into the classroom. You need to take charge of your own life, then you can control these young people."

"Oh, it's not my family trouble that makes me weak in the classroom. I know that my home problem will end with my husband's return, even though it's difficult for me now for him to be away. And, Mr. Gilliam, there is no doubt in my mind that the Lord will move upon these young people to teach them to love Him. Then we teachers will have a better day."

"You're right," he remarked. "The Lord will move upon our youth to bring a better day, but it won't take place until heaven begins."

His words cut into me like a knife, but I knew I spoke truth. Again, I tried to defend myself with a promise to do better. I left his office so distraught that I felt I must go to the bathroom to cry, but he followed me, making it imperative that I swallow my tears and return to my classroom.

I walked into my classroom every day determined to be in control. Oftentimes the children became talkative and refused to settle down to work. It seemed the only way to control them was to raise my voice. The principal had told me several times that I must get tough. But I knew my behavior didn't correspond to my Christian life.

I asked daily to become a better teacher, but the main thrust of my prayers was that my God would stop Duane's romance and bring him home. I saw his return as the answer to every problem. It would bring revival to the school, making it easy to control young people.

To my great sorrow, my miracle-working God didn't answer my prayers and end Duane's new relationship. Within months, Vonda, and Tami, when she came home for the summer, reported to me that Duane and Jo saw each other often, and they suspected romance. That news drove me to take matters into my own hands. I first checked with the girls to get their opinion.

"Do you think I should visit your dad? I fear he cares for Jo because he's alone. Perhaps an evening with me would restore his feelings and awaken a desire for his family."

"It might be wise," Tami said, and Vonda nodded in agreement.

"Good! I'll go tonight. This circumstance calls for immediate action. You girls find me something to wear while I take a bath."

Within a few minutes I was in my car on the way to Duane's house. Softly falling rain set the stage for our meeting. I hurried from the car to his porch. In response to my knock, this man I adored opened the door dressed in khaki pants with no shirt. At sight of him, the old familiar feeling crowded into my heart.

"Hi, Duane! Could I talk to you for a few minutes?" To be with him made it seem almost impossible that we were no longer together. This visit must end our estrangement.

"I suppose so." Silently and indifferently, he returned to his recliner, and I sat in a chair opposite his.

"Do you like living here by yourself?" My mind worked feverishly to come up with a way to penetrate his cold exterior.

"Not particularly, but I'm happier than when I lived with you." He kept his eyes glued to the television.

"How can you say that?" I scooted to the edge of my chair to be closer to him. "I tried to be a good wife. I loved you when we were together, and I love you now. I did my best to please you."

"No, you didn't." He spoke in the same manner that he had used in our old disagreements.

"You placed a church ahead of me. You refused to allow me to be the head of the house, which is my rightful place. I can't live under the conditions your lifestyle dictates." He continued to look at the television, carefully avoiding my eyes.

"You don't have to live like me, Duane. All I ask is freedom to worship as I please. Even our nation gives freedom of worship. Surely you could give me that privilege."

"We gain nothing in discussing our differences. We have said all this before. You're not going to change, and neither am I. You've chosen a new life for yourself." For the first time, he looked straight at me and spoke with loathing, "Everybody says you look sick. I think you're ill."

His words pierced me to the quick. My pretty outfit and the hairdo Tami had given me were in vain. I knew he hated my pale face with no lipstick. But the real hurt came from the thought that in comparison to his new sweetheart, thirteen years my junior, perhaps I did look horrible. I defended myself, "I feel wonderful! I've never felt better in my life."

He rose to his feet and spoke without a trace of emotion. "It's time for you to go. This discussion simply wastes our time."

Reluctantly, I stood and walked with him to the door. As we stood there together, an insatiable longing flooded my heart. Placing my hands on his bare waist, I looked into his face and pled, "Duane, I love you, and I want you to come home. I miss you. I can hardly stand life without you. Please kiss me and tell me that you love me, too."

For a fleeting moment, an indescribable look came into his eyes; then it disappeared. He spoke again in the same cold voice. "You need to go."

I ran to the car in the still-falling rain and began the drive home with another fracture in my already badly damaged heart. Tears streamed from my eyes, nearly blinding me. I talked to my Saviour all the way home.

"I thought I could win him, Jesus. I've thought for years I could gain his affection, but after tonight, I know it's not going to happen soon. I feel I can't wait a moment longer for him to come home. I know I must trust You. Your plan does call for him to come back, doesn't it? I can wait for him, even though I don't want to, but he must come back. I can't live without him."

It rained all the way home, as if heaven cried with me in my heartbreak. The awful look in Duane's eyes when I asked him to kiss me and tell me he loved me kept flashing before my mind. "For just a few brief seconds he considered surrendering to You, Jesus, then the mighty foe won again. You're the reason he doesn't want me anymore. He sees You in me, and he wants no part of Your abundant life, because he would have to give up his worldly life.

"He's a hard man, but that's nothing to You. You softened the heart of King Nebuchadnezzar! You brought King David to his knees! You slapped the Apostle Paul down on the Damascus Road. You want Duane just as much as You wanted these men. You won't give up on him, will You, Jesus? You paid a price for His life. He belongs to You, and You'll use every power of heaven to win him to Yourself. I can trust You to save him!"

A few days later I stood in the front yard as the postman stopped at my mailbox. To my surprise, he stepped from his vehicle to give me an envelope. "Who could be sending you registered mail?"

"I can't imagine." I signed his form and thanked him, then ran into the house. Tearing open the envelope, I read a letter that sent shock waves through my whole body. "Vonda, this is a notification of divorce proceedings. Why would your dad want a divorce? Why would he want to finalize our separation?" I shook my head in disbelief.

"I have no idea, but it might as well happen. He's gone."

"I don't want a divorce, and I don't intend to have one." Taking the telephone directory from the shelf, I picked a name from the list of lawyers and made a call. In answer to my question, the lawyer said, "Your husband has filed for divorce, so you're forced to respond. You'll have to hire a lawyer to plead your case, or you'll lose everything."

I turned back to Vonda. "It looks as if I'll have a divorce whether I want one or not. What a battle your dad fights! He divorces me to prove that he's right and I'm wrong."

The Valley 137

"I know you're right, Mom. Daddy fights a losing battle."

"Thank you for supporting me, honey. I'm so glad to have you girls with me in the faith."

A few days later, my wonderful Lord poured another blessing upon me to lift my injured spirit. Vonda determined to walk in perfect obedience by being baptized and joining the church. Her baptism took place on a Sabbath afternoon, with her sisters and many of our friends coming for the service.

That evening, she brought more happiness to me as she requested of her sisters, "Lori and Tami, please help me carry my television to the garage."

"Why put it in the garage?" Tami asked. "If you don't want it, sell it."

"Daddy gave it to me, and I want to give it back to him. In the meantime, I'm a baptized Christian, and I don't want a television in my bedroom."

The three girls performed the task, then returned to the living room. I walked to the center of the room to make a speech.

"I feel like Elijah, who had power in prayer to call down fire on a flooded sacrifice. The people turned from Baal, to cry, 'The Lord, He is the God! The Lord, He is the God' [1 Kings 18:39]. I have claimed God's promises with prayer and fasting; I have eaten no goodies for several years. Look at the blessings! Four of us have turned from the world to cry, 'The Lord, He is the God!' Kneel with me to pray that your daddy will be brought in soon. He surely stands on his last leg!" The girls and I knelt in a circle in the living room, and I led in prayer.

15

The Valley Deepens

January brought two sad happenings—the first being the death of my daddy, and the second a day in court to become officially divorced.

The notification of divorce made my faith tremble. To realize that Duane actually wanted legal separation seemed unbelievable. As I drove to the court, I repeated a promise that I had claimed daily since before Duane left: "You have a use for Duane and me, and our girls, and You are well-pleased because I make high demands upon You that we may glorify Your name" (adapted from *The Desire of Ages*, page 668).

"I'm making high demands upon You, Jesus, because I want my whole family to uplift Your truth in this dark world. You must bring Duane back to us to make that promise come true. It seems like defeat today, but I have trusted You through this whole ordeal. I must not give up now. The divorce may be the darkness just before the dawn."

Joy rose in my heart a few minutes later as I walked

into a corridor of the court and discovered Duane standing near a window by himself. Sensing the prospect of ending this whole course of action, I hurried to his side with my entreaty, "I love you, Duane. Please stop these divorce proceedings and come home."

His cold answer crushed me. "I want no part of you. Divorce is a necessary step to take you out of my life. I don't want to talk about it again."

Refusing to accept his negative words, I pled, "We must try together to find the root of the trouble, and then we can start over."

He ignored me and quickly walked away. I followed, but was greatly disappointed when he turned a corner and disappeared. Since I had no idea where he had gone, I walked to the waiting room, where I sat beside my lawyer until we could go before the judge.

Duane and his lawyer came into the room a few moments later just as the receptionist said, "We're behind schedule. Your appointment will have to be after lunch."

I jumped up and ran to Duane. "This is a perfect time for us. Please, let's eat lunch together to talk about our difficulty. Our problems can be settled without a divorce." Desperation made me feel that he must agree to my suggestion.

But he had no such sentiment. "Absolutely not! I'll be back after lunch." He stood immediately and left the room.

Since I had no desire to eat, I stayed in the waiting room by myself. Everybody returned at the end of the lunch hour; then Duane and I and our lawyers went in before the judge.

The Valley Deepens 141

"What is the reason for the divorce?" the judge asked.

I kept perfectly quiet, but Duane answered immediately. "We haven't gotten along for seven years. I've lived by myself for more than a year. We're totally incompatible."

His words pierced my heart. I wanted to scream to all of them, "We don't want a divorce. There's no real reason for our perfectly good home to be torn apart. We could get along if he would only talk to me."

The judge hit his gavel on the desk while making the cruel announcement, "I pronounce Duane and Donna Nicholas divorced."

As we stepped out of the judge's chamber, I grabbed Duane's arm in a last frantic effort to salvage our broken relationship. Once again I begged, "Please, Duane, go with me somewhere to discuss our problems." I clung to him, but he pushed me aside and walked away.

Everything in me longed to follow him, but my lawyer called to me, and in a daze, I went to him. Waves of despair rolled over my body as I signed papers that officially cut Duane from my life. Then I walked to the car and drove home. All the way, I talked to my Lord.

"It hurts so much, Jesus. A decree bound us together, and now a decree sets us free, but I don't want to be free. When Duane left, I was sure You allowed it to convert him, but now my faith wavers. In spite of this divorce, I must keep believing that this legal separation will bring him to You, but I'm so scared.

"I need you today, sweet Lord. You're my Brother, interceding for me before the Father. Give me Your love to replace the love my husband refuses to give me. I love him intensely, but teach me to love You so it won't hurt so badly."

The ensuing days made me realize the horror of divorce. Our separation had brought pain, but divorce seemed to have actually cut a piece of flesh from my heart. God had united Duane and me in marriage, and now a worldly judge had ended our union, making my heart throb with an inconsolable hurt.

About two months later, I heard the front door slam, signaling Vonda's return from her job at the nearby ice cream store. "Come to the kitchen," I called to her. "I have exciting news."

She immediately came to sit at a chair by the table, while I washed and sorted beans at the sink. "Tell me your news, Mom, then I'll tell you my news. After spending last night with Daddy, I have something important to tell you."

"I'm eager to hear what's going on in your dad's life, but listen to this miracle God has performed for our school. A few months ago, I talked to Mr. Gilliam about the possibility of making Parkview a four-grade high school. As principal, he informed me that economics made it impossible; however, several of us have continued to pray for this impossibility. At the board meeting last night, the members voted to make it happen. They plan to add an eleventh grade next fall and the twelfth grade the following year—right on time for you and your classmates. What do you think of that?"

"Oh, Mom, how exciting!" Vonda stood up and clapped her hands. "That ends my dilemma about where to go next year. I can graduate with my classmates and stay here two more years. I'm not ready to leave home."

"And I'm not ready for you to leave, honey. The Lord knows I need you, so He moved a mountain for us. But there's more. Since I have both elementary and business education certificates, Mr. Gilliam offered me the position of business teacher and librarian. He thinks I'll have far fewer discipline problems with older youth. After three years of struggling to control elementary children, I'm excited to redeem myself with the challenge of teaching academy youth to love Jesus. Now tell me your news."

A serious look replaced Vonda's smile. "What I have to tell you isn't good news. I decided to ask Daddy if his relationship with Jo was anything more than friendship. He answered, 'At first, I liked her as a friend, but now I love her.' So, Mom, the prayer power that performed a miracle for the school must now be placed on Daddy. You know what follows romance."

My bubble of happiness burst. The school blessing faded in light of another woman in my man's life. I knew that if Vonda realized how the negative news about Duane hurt me, she would never tell me anything, so I maintained my composure and calmly answered, "I've been afraid their affair might become serious, but the miracle at school proves the power of prayer. With God's help, I proclaim the destiny of their togetherness to be ashes!"

"I hope you're right. Daddy couldn't marry until your divorce is final anyway. When is he free?" Vonda asked.

"There's a six-month waiting period, so he must wait four more months. But, honey, he can't really be in love with Jo. Your dad has to still love me. He's just lonely."

"At least he thinks he loves her," Vonda answered.

"I'm going to take a walk to talk to the Lord about all these things." I placed a lid on the beans, turned the fire on low, and went to my room to don my jogging suit. Pain returned in greater intensity than ever as I cried all the way to my altar.

With anguish and fear in my heart, I knelt to pray: "Father, why have You allowed him to think he's in love with her? You have all power. You can change his feelings. Please don't let him keep loving her. Please don't let him touch her. Surely You won't allow him to marry this woman. Your promises have proven that You plan to save him and return him to our home. Bring him soon, Father. I love him, and I feel I can't live without him.

"I surrender my life anew to You right now. Take every sin away. You know my weakness—help me overcome so I can have power in prayer. I shall add another fast to my renewed commitment. You sent an impression not long ago that I should eat only two meals each day. From now on, I'll eat only two meals with no snacking. You and I have a covenant, Father. I change my eating habits—You save my darling husband.

"I claim the prayer of Jehoshaphat. This divorce is the great multitude coming against me. I set myself to fast and pray, even as he sought You earnestly. And You sent the wonderful assurance to him:

"'Be not afraid nor dismayed by reason of this great multitude; for the battle is not yours, but God's. Ye shall not need to fight in this battle: set yourselves, stand ye still, and see the salvation of the Lord with you, O Judah and Jerusalem: fear not, nor be dismayed;

tomorrow go out against them: for the Lord will be with you.'" 2 Chronicles 20:15, 17.

I rose from my knees spiritually strong. God's Word told me that He held my wandering husband's life in His hands, and prayer would restore my home.

Only a few days later, I happened to be standing outside when Duane arrived in his new Oldsmobile to get Vonda. Without a thought, I ran to the passenger side, opened the door, and leaned close to him. Looking directly into his eyes, I spoke very tenderly. "You have a beautiful new car. I still love you, Duane."

At that moment Vonda came bounding from the house. I had to pull back from the car, giving no time for his response, so she could jump in. They drove away, taking my heart with them.

I walked into the house, mourning the fact that he had a beautiful new car, a handsome face, expensive clothes, and a pretty young girlfriend. "Oh! It hurts too much!" I cried. "I can't bear for him to love her."

My aching heart led me to pray: "You made me a romantic person, Jesus. I have loved Duane all my life. This trial comes because I placed him above You. Today You are first in my affections, but I want to love You much more. Make my devotion to You a force in me, drawing others to You. Let my worship of You sustain me in this trial, so that others will see You in me—and not a sad woman who lost her much-loved husband."

I spent the next weekend with my mother. On Sunday morning, she and I attended her Methodist church. While the pastor preached, I looked at the beautiful portrait of Christ above the choir loft. I seemed to hear words from heaven: "You've been to Gethsemane—now you're going on to Calvary."

"What does that mean?" I asked my Lord, but I heard no answer. I pondered the words all day as Mother and I talked. "Surely, I've suffered enough," I thought to myself. "Victory must be next on the agenda. It can't be Calvary."

16

Gethsemane

The summer of 1983 became a time of mental and spiritual growth for me. I took a class in library science at Central State University in Edmond in preparation for the position as librarian at Parkview. In spite of all the studying involved with the class, I found much time for Bible study and prayer.

Week after week, it seemed that the Lord led me to fast and pray—one day a week, two days a week, and twice I felt impressed to fast for three days. My human nature often rebelled when the call came to deny myself food, but during these weeks as the presence of Jesus grew ever more real, fasting became easier. I felt on the verge of a miracle. I sensed power with the Lord, and held every prayer request before Him daily, but I prayed for Duane constantly.

My faith grew until I seemed to be flying. Often I returned from seasons of prayer on the campus expecting to see Duane's car in the driveway. I knew he was probably spending time with Jo, yet my mind overflowed with thoughts of the two of us getting married again. Like the

Apostle Paul who fasted for three days at the home of Ananias before he began his powerful ministry, I knew something big lay before me. I couldn't help but dream that Duane could be dramatically converted like Paul, and the two of us could begin our great work.

Midway through summer college classes, Mother and I spent the weekend with my sister Lois and her husband in Bartlesville. I left their house early on Sunday morning to walk to a nearby school campus, where I found a special spot. There the Lord rewarded my weeks of seeking after Him by pouring the Holy Spirit upon my prayer. Requests flowed from my lips for family, friends, and school, and especially for Duane: "Let him see the girls and me in heaven with You. Make him sense the horror of being left out. Then show him You have borne his sin and long to renew his salvation."

The great power I felt in prayer proved to me that victory was near. I felt exalted for the remainder of the weekend. Gone were the words I had only recently heard: "Now you're going on to Calvary."

My summer library class ended, and the fall term at the academy began. With my new teaching position in the high school with more mature youth, a new hope filled my heart. I determined to end my problems with discipline by practicing good control in my classroom. Most of all, I desired to bring the young people to a burning love for Jesus, which would be the goal of my devotions at the beginning of every class and the morning worship for the whole upper-grade student body every fifth week.

During the first week that I had charge of the joint worship, I shared my prayer experience in Bartlesville,

Gethsemane 149

beginning with a quotation that had increased my faith: "'We must not only pray in Christ's name, but by the inspiration of the Holy Spirit . . . When with earnestness and intensity we breathe a prayer in the name of Christ, there is in that very intensity a pledge from God that He is about to answer our prayer exceeding abundantly above all that we ask or think' [*Christ's Object Lessons*, page 147].

"The intensity I felt in prayer," I continued, "is a pledge that God is about to answer my prayer. That promise means my ex-husband will soon be converted and return home. For this school and everybody on my prayer list, the pledge assures us of capturing a love for Jesus that will turn the world upside down."

I ended my presentation by inviting the young people to join me under the big tree east of the gymnasium at noon every day for prayer. Since my second year at Parkview, I had sponsored a prayer time for students during the thirty-minute lunch break. Young children were my most frequent visitors, but on this day David and Kirk, seventh- and eighth-graders, surprised me with their attendance. As they sat on the blanket I had spread on the ground, Kirk said, "I remember when we were in your fifth- and sixth-grade classroom, you fasted from sweets for your husband to be saved. Do you still not eat goodies?"

"I've continued that fast for several years to strengthen my prayer that God will save my husband. But I want more than his salvation; I want to lead our people to revival—to show them how wonderful the Lord is. He must have leaders to accomplish His work, and perhaps you two young men are the very ones He can use on this campus."

While I spoke, I opened my Bible and handed it to David. "Please read Nehemiah 2:20 for our prayer promise."

David read the words: "Then answered I them, and said unto them, The God of heaven, He will prosper us; therefore we His servants will arise and build."

We knelt, and I prayed that God would make the three of us like Nehemiah to lead the youth of Parkview to know the Lord. David spoke a short prayer; then Kirk made me smile with his words: "Please send Mrs. Nicholas' husband home soon so she can eat candy."

The new buoyancy in my faith couldn't erase the heartbreaking events approaching with the holiday season. On Thanksgiving the girls and I met my brother and sisters and their families at my mother's home. I loved such gatherings, but this year a cloud hung over my enjoyment. Duane had taken Jo to his family gathering at his aunt's home only a few miles away.

Several times throughout the day, I slipped to the bathroom to lock the door and kneel to pray. "Father, she's mixing with Duane's family as I've done for years and should still be doing. Why do You allow it? Why do You let him go on playing this game, when in heaven's records he's still married to me? You've promised me that he's coming back. I've been thinking positive thoughts of our life together again, but with this happening, I've regressed to heartbreak again. I can't stand for her to be with my man."

For a few moments, I enjoyed the luxury of tears; then I continued my prayer. "Make Duane realize he has no right to this woman. Make him remember my love—a love like Your love, that keeps on loving in spite of terrible treatment." I cried again, then I carefully dried my eyes. I must keep in control. My family knew that my religion had caused our broken home. Because they felt that my belief bordered on fanaticism, I carefully hid my feelings while I was in their presence, to act as if everything were lovely. Inside, a horrible fear welled up that my faith couldn't remove. Could my present experience be only a Gethsemane? Could going on to Calvary mean that my Lord would allow Duane to marry?

For several days I experienced intense heartbreak, but again the Lord led me to fast and pray. My faith returned in full force. This was the darkness before the dawn. Christmas would bring the exceeding abundant answer of a restored home. The anticipation of this event soothed my hurting heart.

Tami, Vonda, and I again went to my mother's home on Christmas Eve. As we sat in the living room, watching the fire dance in the fireplace, Lori arrived, loaded with packages. "Hi, everybody! Sorry to be late, but I stopped to see Granddad and Grandma Nicholas. Dad and Jo were there, so I stayed longer than I intended."

I felt an awful foreboding. In spite of a wobbling chin, I tried to speak calmly. "Lori, are they staying all night?"

"Yes," she answered. "And Grandma wants us girls to come sometime tomorrow so we can all be together."

"It sounds to me like Duane has a romance in his life," Mother said, as Lori's news penetrated her mind. "Honey, what have I told you? If you don't give up this crazy religion, he'll find a new wife. A home is God's highest institution. Your home remains broken because you can't be satisfied with the faith you've had all your life. And it's Christmas, when families should be together. It breaks my heart, Donna."

I struggled to hold back tears and remain calm. "I know, Mom. Duane's relationship with Jo scares me, but obedience to the heavenly Father comes first, whatever the cost."

"You were obedient to God as a Methodist," Mother answered. "This trouble coming upon you means you must be following Satan. Let's not talk about this any more. Such feelings spoil our Christmas."

"Good idea! Vonda, pass out the presents. I can't wait to see what's in all those pretty packages." Mother's words added more pain to my bleeding heart, but I smiled and acted happy. Finally bedtime came, and with relief I buried my face in a pillow and cried.

Soon after Christmas Lori decided to tell me the rest of the story. She and I had gone to the campus for a walk when she broke the awful news: "I hate to tell you this, Mom, but you might as well know. Dad gave Jo a ring for Christmas which proves he thinks he loves her."

I was immediately taken aback and stopped to face my daughter. "It surprises me, although with all that's happened, I shouldn't be bowled over by anything. This proves again that the relationship has become serious. But, honey, I've held countless promises before the Lord. I can't think He will allow your dad to marry."

"I hope you're right, Mom, and I think you are. Your prayers are pretty powerful." We spoke no more of Duane as we returned to the house.

After school resumed, Vonda dashed into the library

to see me on Thursday morning after spending the night with her dad. She leaned over my desk in her eagerness to make sure I understood her words. "Daddy and Jo bought a beautiful home. Because the house needs repair, they got a special price. They plan to start work on it immediately. Mom, the signs loom ominous for a wedding—first a ring, and now a home."

I put my hands to my throat, then pulled them away. "These happenings frighten me, but I trust the Lord."

"I'm glad you keep faith, Mom. I wouldn't believe for a victory if it weren't for you, but I think you're right. The Lord surely won't let Daddy marry Jo." Vonda stood up to leave, then turned back to hear my final words: "I see a much greater victory in God allowing the wedding plans, then making Duane fall flat on his face before Him, confess his sin, and rise up a new man in Christ, ready to proclaim salvation. That kind of miracle would grip the attention of everyone."

"Spoken like my mom; I believe you," Vonda said with a trusting smile, then left for class.

The hurt continued, but hope in an exceeding abundant answer stayed in my heart. Every morning, I talked to my heavenly Father: "When heaven begins, I'm going to consider this trial a cheap price to pay for entrance, but today it hurts pretty badly. This is the night of weeping. Hasten the morning of joy!"

Two months later, I stood at my car door on a Thursday morning when Duane brought Vonda to school after she had spent the night with him. Happy to see him, I smiled and waved. He gave me a short wave in return, then drove away.

Vonda followed me to the library. The look on her face told me she had momentous news. "Listen to this, Mom. Daddy told me he and Jo plan to get married. I asked him on the way to school this morning what date they had set for the wedding, and he said, 'Tomorrow.' Mom, Daddy and Jo plan to get married tomorrow, Friday."

I stared at my daughter in disbelief. The joy of seeing Duane evaporated as I tried to comprehend her words. Then, just as quickly, I knew the answer. "Oh, honey, he's teasing you. Instead of actually telling you the date he plans to get married, he said, 'Tomorrow.' That's just like your dad. However, I've reconciled myself to the fact that he plans to get married. I feel almost positive God won't allow them to marry. If by one chance in a thousand, He permits a wedding, I have to know Duane's marriage is part of God's plan for us. This gives me a great story for my worship talk this morning, doesn't it?"

"You may have to eat your words," Vonda answered.

Thirty minutes later, we gathered in the classroom for worship. All week I had been using Exodus 14 and 15 for my theme. On this Thursday morning, I continued by bringing the Scripture to my own experience: "Moses led the children of Israel from Egyptian bondage to the Promised Land. They stood at the Red Sea, with the raging water in front of them, mountains on each side, Pharaoh's army in hot pursuit, and no way of escape. The thought came to these terrified people that Moses had led them from bondage to be either destroyed or taken captive again.

"This morning I stand before you students in a circumstance like that of Moses. The Lord has led me from Egyptian captivity to the world, to follow Him in an exciting relationship. Just as Moses walked with God in perfect communion, performing miracles in calling down plagues and in bringing over a million people out of Egypt, so I have developed a living relationship with the Lord. He has answered many prayers for me—He saved my children, He turned our junior academy into a senior academy, and I see His power constantly in my daily life.

"Today I seek Him for a miracle as big as parting the Red Sea. I want my husband to become a converted Seventh-day Adventist and be home with us again. Vonda informs me this morning that her dad told her he plans marriage soon. It shook me just a little to hear that news, even though I've been expecting it. It also makes me realize Moses might have had a doubt when he looked at that raging sea in front of him and saw the dust of Pharaoh's army behind, but he didn't allow appearances to shake his faith. He said to his people, 'Stand still, and see the salvation of the Lord, which He will shew to you today, for the Egyptians whom ye have seen today, ye shall see them again no more forever. The Lord shall fight for you and ye shall hold your peace' [Exodus 14:13, 14].

"You know what happened? They walked through the Red Sea on dry ground. Pharaoh's army followed and were drowned. In my situation, I repeat Moses' words, 'Stand still and see the salvation of the Lord.' I have sought the Lord with fasting and prayer for this husband and father. Appearances can't defeat our faith. Ninety-nine chances out of one hundred tell us the mighty heavenly Father intervenes to stop this planned wedding.

However, one chance says God may have a better plan. Either way, we see His salvation exalted while He fights this battle for us."

The students listened attentively. How I loved talking to them about the Lord!

The great miracle I expected would impact their faith; it would bring the revival. As I taught classes the remainder of the day, my own faith grew. Victory was near!

17

Calvary

After a busy weekend, I went to bed early on Monday night. Vonda awakened me with a shake of my shoulder. "Mom, can you get up? Tami wants to talk to you."

"Oh, I was sound asleep. What time is it?" I rubbed my eyes and threw back the covers.

"It's 10:00. I'm ready to go to bed, too, but I'm going to hear what Tami has to say." She stopped by her room, and I went to the kitchen phone.

"Hello, Tami. I guess you know you got me out of bed."

"Mom, are you sitting down?" she asked, ignoring my reproach.

"Yes, I am now." I unsuspectingly moved to sit in the chair beside the phone.

"I called Dad a few minutes ago to tell him about my teaching position for next year. He said, 'I've been meaning to call you.' I asked him, 'Why?'" Tami paused as though struggling for words. Then she continued in an emotion-packed voice, "Dad said, 'Jo and I got married Friday.'" She paused again, then exclaimed, "Mom, Dad got married!"

Stunned by my daughter's words, I stood to my feet with an awful sinking feeling inside.

Tears immediately made their way down my cheeks. "No! Oh, no! It can't be true! God can't allow your dad to marry Jo."

"Mom, do you remember that he told me last Thursday that he planned to get married tomorrow?" Vonda asked from the phone in her room. "When I told you, you said he was teasing me. This proves the truth of his words."

I numbly walked back and forth in front of the phone, pinching myself to make sure I was awake. "He meant it for sure. I simply refused to admit it."

"It shocks me," Tami said. "You convinced all of us he wouldn't marry. I can't understand why God allowed it to happen when you prayed so earnestly."

"I don't understand it either, honey." I grabbed a tissue from the box on the cabinet and vigorously blew my nose. "From the day your dad left, I believed he would be back. I told our family and friends countless times, 'The Lord will bring Duane back to us.' I didn't make idle remarks. I backed my words with Scripture promises and with fasting and prayer."

"Even the kids at school think Daddy's coming home," Vonda added.

"I thought I could pray him home. With Jo wearing a

Calvary 159

ring and the two of them buying a house, which would be enough to make any normal person give up, my faith clung to the dream that the Lord would pull him away from her, convert him, and return him to me." I paused to cry aloud. "My faith gave me confidence that the Lord planned to make everything beautiful in His time. Why am I such a dreamer, girls? Do I just refuse to believe what I don't want to happen?"

"Mom, you want good things, and you pray in faith. I don't understand why God didn't reward your trust," Vonda replied sympathetically.

I took a deep breath and tried to answer calmly. "Honey, I must admit I could never sense perfect assurance that your dad wouldn't marry Jo. Since he has married her, I know this has to be God's answer to us, even though I don't like the answer."

"I know we have to keep faith," Tami responded, "but I surely don't see how this is best. I'd like to talk to you all night, but I have to teach school tomorrow. I must hang up."

"Let's unite our hearts in prayer before we say goodbye," I suggested. "With your dad on a honeymoon with a young bride, we certainly need the Lord." The word *honeymoon* caused me to break down again, but I calmed myself, knelt beside the chair, and prayed into the phone, "Father, this is Your production, but we don't understand the script You have given us tonight. It ruins our happiness, our hopes, our dreams, everything! I told You I could tolerate the marriage if it was in Your will, but I can't. It's too much for me, and it's too much for these girls. You must give us faith to pierce this blackness."

We hung up the phones, and Vonda hurried to join me in the kitchen. "This is just awful, Mom." She put her arms around me, and we stood crying together. Then she reminded me, "We must call Lori. She'll want to know."

"Go to your phone again," I said. "I'll dial her number, and you can tell her."

A sleepy-sounding Lori answered the phone a moment later. "Why are you calling me this time of night?"

We repeated the sad news of the conversation with Tami. She expressed the same disbelief, grief, and disappointment. We shared for several minutes; then with Lori's promise to come home after she dismissed her students from school on Friday, we hung up the phones. I hugged Vonda, and the two of us went to our separate bedrooms.

All night I cried and prayed and questioned God's leading. Only recently I had read: "The Lord brings His children over the same ground again and again . . . until they are in harmony with Christ." *My Life Today*, page 92. I wondered if this could be my experience. Jesus had carried me through each step of my ex-husband's romance. Every event had hurt unbearably, yet as the Lord had gotten me through these tight spots, I had learned to endure pain I had never dreamed possible.

But marriage seemed too much. "They live together all day long. She prepares his meals. She washes his clothes. They make love. He shares his whole life with her just as he shared it with me. It is sickening, unbearable, horrible! I could easily look on his body in a casket, but I can't stand for him to be married to someone else."

Before my girls, I had managed to keep my feelings partially under control, but in my bedroom, I surrendered to the anguish that filled my heart. I cried aloud until I could cry no more; then I turned to the Lord. "Jesus, please come and place Your arms around me. My faith died tonight. I didn't think my heart could hurt more, but it feels like a running sore. The man I have dearly loved since I was twelve, who loved me just as much, is now in the arms of a pretty young woman while I live alone. I feel completely forsaken."

Finally I went to sleep. When I awakened, it was too late for my usual prayer time on the campus, so Vonda and I ate a small breakfast and went straight to school. All day I taught, while my mind stayed on the marriage. Many times I asked the Lord, "How can I tell these young people that my fondest dream is crushed? I told them You were going to part the Red Sea to save Duane. Instead, I'm drowning in the waves with Pharaoh and his army."

Lori called almost as soon as Vonda and I got home that evening. "How was your day, Mom?"

"I had a terrible day. The Lord's purpose in this situation completely baffles me. I couldn't bring myself to tell the students or the teachers about the marriage."

"That brings up a question. You have convinced all our family and friends that God will bring Dad home—how are you going to tell them about this disappointment without weakening their belief?" Lori's tone of voice spoke clearly of her own misgivings.

From the phone in her room, Vonda added her skepticism. "With this kind of example, we can't expect to win any of our family to our church. Who would want to serve a God who doesn't answer such a prayer as you prayed?"

My two daughters' doubting words renewed my own faith. "Girls, we must not be so foolish as to give up and let Satan win the battle because the plan doesn't fit our ideas. The Lord allowed the marriage. He says 'No' to many prayers. I can pray with the Psalmist, 'He hath smitten my life down to the ground,' but he goes on to say, 'My soul thirsteth after Thee' [Psalm 143:3, 6]. I know I must seek the Lord with every fiber of my being and let Him handle Duane.

"We walk on hot coals right now. Since God allowed the marriage, we must gain victory over our feelings. In fact, I'll go to my altar to pray as soon as we stop this conversation. The three of us and Tami have never stood in such need of prayer as now."

"OK, Mom," Lori answered, "I'll hang up so you can go pray. I'll call again soon."

Leaving Vonda at the house, I ran to the campus to seek the Lord. Kneeling at my Storm the Gates of Heaven Altar, I earnestly prayed, "Sweet Jesus, the girls and I struggle with this crisis. I try to encourage them so they won't lose faith, but I need my own support. Show me today what I can believe. The dearest treasure of my life is in another's arms this evening. Take away my longing for him and give me a desire for only You."

The Lord carried me through the next two days. I hardly felt His presence, but gradually He penetrated my hurt with comfort and the knowledge that I had a responsibility to my daughters and to my students. With a reputation

Calvary 163

among these young people as a woman of strong faith, I must prove I could stand the pressure of a severe trial.

On Friday morning I became very intense as I went to my campus altar. "I'm in a tight spot, dear Father. I know I've been sinful to allow ugly thoughts to fill my mind, when this marriage may be the very step that brings Duane to salvation. And perhaps this is the test I need to prove I can be victorious over self and in perfect harmony with You. I cannot be so weak as to fail You, no matter what the test may be. I must continue to pray the prayer of Moses when he stood at the Red Sea: 'Fear ye not, stand still and see the salvation of the Lord, which He will shew to you today: for the Egyptians whom ye have seen today, ye shall see them again no more for ever. The Lord shall fight for you, and ye shall hold your peace' [Exodus 14:13-14].

"I truly want to seek You with every fiber of my being and let You fight the battle with Duane. At the same time, fill me with the power of Your Holy Spirit and Your love. I'm sick of people loving the world more than they love You—the kids at school, my fellow church members, my family, my friends, everyone. In this heartbreaking experience, make me represent Your character so these people will be drawn to love You.

A blessed assurance flowed over me that God had everything under control. I rose from my knees with love for God flooding my soul. I looked at the brilliant blue sky and praised His name as I ran all the way to the house to get ready for another day of school.

Standing before the ninth-grade typing class, I began my worship talk. "You remember, young people, that one week ago today I presented a dilemma facing my girls and me. Vonda returned from spending the night with her father to tell me he planned to marry soon. On hearing this news, my faith barely flinched. For more than two years, I had claimed God's promises for my ex-husband to find salvation and return home. I simply looked to heaven and prayed, 'Father, I'm expecting a miracle to prevent this wedding.'"

I gazed at the students to gain their full attention before I continued with my story.

"Duane married his sweetheart last Friday, the very day I told you God wouldn't allow it. Since I fully believed my prayers could prevent this wedding, it has been quite a setback. Temptation assails me constantly. 'Why don't you quit believing in spectacular manifestations of God's power? Why don't you act like an ordinary Christian? God doesn't give you any more than He gives others who don't proclaim strong faith.'"

On hearing these words, David Birth looked at me, shocked. "Mrs. Nicholas, you can't give up. You can't ever give up on Jesus."

"Thank you, David. I needed to hear those words. And I can tell you, I'm not going to give up. I don't understand the way my Lord works, but I know I can trust Him. I felt low in faith when I got up this morning, but I sought Jesus at my campus altar before I came to school. He lifted my spirits.

"I realized that this experience has been an answer to my prayer to know the love of Jesus. Jesus said to His disciples many times, 'I will be crucified and rise again the third day,' just as I have told you young people and many others, 'The Lord will bring Duane back to me.'

"As the weight of guilt pressed upon the Saviour, as He felt the heartbreaking disappointment of being shut out of heaven forever, so Duane's marriage brought the disappointment to me that he is gone from me forever.

"Jesus must have cried out, 'Father, You let Me believe a lie from eternity. Why did You let me think I could come through victoriously?' Those are my exact feelings, as I have asked the Father over and over, 'Why did you send reassurances to me? Why have You let me believe this when You knew it wouldn't come true?'

"Now listen to this unbelievable story. Satan came with his temptation to Jesus to give it up because it was going to cost His eternal life. Jesus thought of the consequences—He would plunge into nothingness, never to be in heaven with His Father again. He thought of you and me, weak sinful human beings, who would die eternally without His sacrifice. He made His decision because He loved us more than He loved Himself. 'Satan, get behind Me. I'll die that they might live.'

"Jesus willingly laid down His life for me. How could I not love Him? How can I complain about my trial, when He did so much for me? He didn't bring Duane back, but 'All things work together for good' [Romans 8:28], so what looks like defeat is simply a better plan in the mind of God.

"We must seek Him to kindle a burning love in our hearts. We must find a zeal that will wean us from the world and set us afire with this message." As I concluded my devotional, I felt almost like my old self again. The pain in my heart continued, but Jesus' presence was with me, and I determined to never let go of Him again.

18

Intercession

For the next fourteen months, I walked closely with the Lord. Duane's marriage shut the door on the possibility of his soon return, allowing the Lord to ease my heartache; however, I comforted myself with the belief that he would one day be with me again. Sometimes Vonda reported activities that brought a pang to my heart: "They spent the weekend with Grandpa and Grandma." "The clerk at the pet store thought they were a sharp-looking couple." "They went on a trip to New Orleans."

Because of his apparent happiness, I often complained, "In spite of all my requests, Jesus, You have given Duane a good life with his sweetheart. It isn't fair. You must bless me with a powerful ministry for Your Kingdom." I made an extra effort to push thoughts of him to the back of my mind while I earnestly sought the Lord for strength to do a greater work in winning young people.

Then Vonda's graduation from Parkview brought a setback. Duane promised he would attend the ceremony along with Jo and her daughter, Jessie. I became anxious at the thought of seeing him with his new family for the first time.

"How do I compare to a woman thirteen years younger?" I asked the girls on the Saturday night of the graduation service. I twirled in my bright pink dress, holding my skirt like a model.

"You look really good, Mom," Lori answered. "Tami outdid herself choosing that dress. And I've combed your hair to look the best ever."

"I hate to look so good. A child of the King must be humble." My new dress and pretty hairdo made me feel as giddy as a schoolgirl. I glanced in the mirror with the thought crossing my mind that Duane would surely think I looked as good as his new wife.

We drove to Central Seventh-day Adventist Church for the scheduled ceremony. Lori, Tami, and I sat close to the front, and within a few minutes they informed me that Duane, Jo, and Jessie had taken seats near the back. The eight seniors marched in to the music of "Pomp and Circumstance," and the program began.

My heart burst with pride as Vonda played a piano solo, sang in a trio, and gave the salutatorian's speech. I prayed that her dad would take note of her accomplishments.

At the close of the service, the class marched out. Soon the ushers dismissed our row, and the girls and I moved to the aisle. Out of the corner of my eye, I saw Duane and his family at the back. I looked straight ahead as we walked up the aisle. When we got to their row, I turned my eyes to smile at my ex-husband, but his face was turned away. To my utter dismay my eyes fell upon Jo, bringing horror to my heart. I could hardly believe that this woman, who was much prettier and much younger than I had imagined, sat beside my former husband. The familiar ache returned. In great distress, I walked on to the fellowship hall for the reception.

For several minutes I covered my feelings and chatted with friends, watching Duane and Jo out of the corner of my eye. The girls stood with them at the side of the room, where they talked and ate refreshments. After a few minutes, an insane desire rose inside me to meet Jo. "I want Duane to have to introduce us," I thought, and without a moment's hesitation, I walked toward their group. He immediately stepped several feet away, leaving the girls to make introductions.

"This is my mom," Tami said to Jo and Jessie.

"I'm so glad to meet you, Donna." Jo smiled as she shook my hand. "You certainly have three sweet daughters, and I've heard such good things about you."

I stiffened my legs to keep them from buckling under me. "Thank you, Jo," I murmured.

"I'm happy to meet you, and I'm happy to meet you, Jessie." Numbness spread through my body, making me know I should never have approached my ex-husband's new wife.

I stood with them for only a moment, then I deliberately walked a few feet behind them to Duane. "Hello, Duane. It's good to see you." My queasy feelings disappeared, leaving me perfectly comfortable with this man with whom I had lived for years.

"Hello, Donna." His face appeared expressionless.

I couldn't bear it. I looked right into his eyes. "You surely did yourself up proud, Duane!"

"What?" he asked.

"You surely did yourself up proud." I felt a sense of confidence as I turned to walk back to where the girls stood with Jo and Jessie. But my assurance again turned to misery as they lined up the three of them with Vonda and began taking pictures. I watched in torment as Lori and Tami stood in some of the pictures, but I managed to keep a smile on my face while my thoughts ran rampant: "The girls shouldn't have their pictures made with this woman and her daughter, Father. They don't belong to Duane. He belongs to us. Oh! How could he have done this terrible thing?"

Soon the cameras were laid aside, and they all said goodbye. Duane, Jo, and Jessie started toward the door. I couldn't bear to see him go. Everything in me cried out, "Duane, come back! We love you! We're your family! Don't go with those people!" But I stood helpless while the one I loved with all my heart walked out of my life again.

Soon we left the church. Vonda went with her class to a graduation party, and I walked to the car with Lori and Tami, not having the slightest idea of the trouble I was in with my two daughters.

"Give me one reason why you came to meet Jo, Mom." Lori's voice conveyed her disgust. She steered the car from the church drive to the main road.

"I felt an uncontrollable urge to meet her. You girls were with the three of them, and I decided Duane should introduce me to his wife and stepdaughter. You noticed that he stepped away when he saw me coming. It was foolish of me; I became weak all over when she shook my hand and told me she had heard good things about me."

"No, you certainly shouldn't have come near us, Mom." Tami now joined her sister in the lecture. "Your actions betrayed that you still love Dad. You should have stayed with your own friends so she wouldn't think you cared."

"Yes, Mom," Lori added, "you need a little sophistication. You have no dignity or pride when it comes to Dad."

My daughters' rebukes, added to the trauma of the evening, proved too much for me. I lost control and put my face in my hands to cry hysterically.

Immediately, Lori apologized. "I'm sorry, Mom. You're a great Christian. You want to do a good work for Jesus, but you can't seem to get past Dad."

"Me, too, Mom," Tami said, as I continued sobbing. "Forgive me for being cruel. I know we can't understand how you feel."

I regained my composure and wiped my eyes. "You girls are right. I think I unconsciously left my Lord at home when I went to the service, and then followed the demands of my human nature to act foolishly. If I had kept my distance from your dad and his new family, I might not feel so sick and sad. It devastated me to see him with Jo and her daughter, bringing everything back as if it had just happened. You girls dressed me beautifully, but I can't compete with her. Tonight knocked me flat on my face."

I knew I couldn't sleep, so after we arrived home, I changed clothes and walked outside. Placing the lawn chair in a reclining position, I sat down and looked into the night sky. "Father, I thought You had healed me, but my heartache has returned in great proportions. I'm still obsessed with Duane. I can't stand to think about him with her.

"I don't understand Your leading, and I'm complaining. Why does he get to live on the mountaintop, and we have to stay in the valley? I have dared to dream all this year that You would move either before or at Vonda's graduation to convert Duane. When Carlos decided to transfer to Ozark Academy to finish his schooling, I begged him to stay so he wouldn't miss the great blessing that I felt positive would take place. It's so disappointing. The devil tempts me to think victory will never come.

"It isn't fair, Father. I've prayed for five years for revival to come to my school, with no success. I've prayed for Duane to come back, and he was there tonight with his new wife, both of them looking like movie stars. Are you going to let me go on babbling forever about big happenings in the spiritual world and never make them come true? I can hardly bear it."

After much complaining and many tears, it seemed the Lord changed my thoughts. Perhaps He had allowed this night's awful happening to give me another picture of Himself. Every day, He sees His people with their worldly treasures, even as I saw Duane with his new love. He holds His nail-scarred hands before the heavenly Father to plead the price He paid on the cross. In response to His prayer, the Holy Spirit woos each person. A few respond to His call, but most walk away. His heart breaks, even as my heart broke tonight to see Duane walk away with his new family.

The awful sin of His people crucifies Jesus afresh. He bore the penalty 2,000 years ago, and now He feels it again when they commit the act. The thought drew a prayer from my lips: "How wonderful You are, Jesus! You cry as Your people walk away from You, then make plans immediately to come again to plead with greater force. You watch constantly for a small sign of repentance, then You stand there to take them back into Your arms.

"I sense a touch of Your love in my feelings for Duane. Forgiving him would be easy if he would come back to me. Since that can't happen now, transfer all my brokenhearted feelings to Yourself so I can realize the broken heart You had at Calvary—and the one You have now too because Your people won't accept Your great salvation."

The insight about my Lord comforted my heart with a renewed zeal for my work for Him. I must somehow find a way to bring more success. With a free summer ahead, I pledged myself to deeper study. The Lord had given the Apostle Paul such a vision of Calvary when He converted him on the Damascus Road, that he was on fire to tell the world of the cross. I reminded the Lord, "I've seen a little more of Calvary tonight. Give me words to tell my world about Your sacrifice."

19

Pursuing the Dream

After several days of renewed heartbreak, I knelt at my altar at the pond to pray. "Father, again I commit Duane to You. Place him at the back of my mind, and anoint me to tell my world about the heartbreak of Jesus."

Suddenly a thrilling insight lifted my spirits. I remembered that the disciples had endured the disappointment of Gethsemane and Calvary, but then had come the thrilling appointment to take the resurrection message to the world. Instantly, I identified my own suffering experience with these men. Now, like them, I sensed that I could look forward to an appointment for a wonderful work. Ecstatic at the prospect of a soon-coming victory, I changed my prayer to grateful praise and hurried home to tell the girls.

After three years of teaching in church schools in Oklahoma, Lori had decided to move to California to work on a master's degree in public health at Loma Linda University. Since I hated for her to move so far away, I now happily informed her, "Lori, I'm sure that the fulfillment of our dreams lies right around the corner. You can't go west. We must keep faith and wait for the victory."

"If a spiritual triumph comes, I won't leave," she promised. Then only a few days later, she brought more encouragement to us with her report of a book she had read—*Living in Our Finest Hour*. "With the power of the Holy Spirit resting upon us, we could win souls like the multitudes who came to Jesus through the disciples' preaching," she said. "In this book, Gordon Cooper challenges us to pray more earnestly for the divine touch. I believe this is the answer!"

The idea to pray intently for heavenly power thrilled the three girls and me as we laid hold of Lori's suggestion. I reminded them, "The disciples turned the world upside down with their ministry. And God promises more power to us to do our work than He gave these men 2,000 years ago. The Saviour must be shown again as far more desirable and worthy of our love than all the treasures of the world. This work, only the Holy Spirit can do!"

In spite of my undying faith for a soon-coming victory, Lori moved to California when the fall term of school began. Tami started a second year of teaching in the Mesquite, Texas, church school, and Vonda began life at Southwestern Adventist College.

I often prayed on the telephone with the three of them for the Lord to pour His Holy Spirit upon us. Every time Tami and Vonda came home from Texas, we prayed for power at my altar. Each time I presented the worship talks throughout that school year, we expected the outpouring. The girls would call at the end of the day to ask, "Did anything happen, Mom?" I always had to admit that the young people left worship to talk about music, movies, and worldly heroes. We continued to wait while we claimed promises with expectant hearts. Daily blessings fell upon us in abundant measure, but the powerful display didn't take place.

During spring break I led the week of prayer for the elementary school in Mesquite, where Tami taught fifth through eighth grades. I wrote five programs from the book of Esther, memorized them, and presented them to the students. I sensed a love for Jesus gripping my heart as I placed these verses in my mind. I told the young people that Jesus went before the heavenly Father with the prayer of Esther on His lips: "I will go in unto the king, and if I perish, I perish." (See Esther 3:16.) As our sin was placed upon Him, He perished, but in His death is the power that enabled Esther to save her people—and power for us to save our people. I tried to motivate the youth to memorize the Word, seek for what it tells about Jesus, then pray the learned verses for love for Him to fill their hearts.

Another insight came to me after the week of prayer. I called each of my daughters to tell them. "Esther didn't rush ahead to her work but obeyed God in putting on a banquet for the king and Haman. In the same way, the Lord has a plan for us, and our long wait proves He has a special banquet in mind. We must keep our eyes on the great Scriptwriter so we won't miss our lines."

Heaven's blessing continued upon me as I returned to my work at Parkview, where it was my week to be in charge of worship for the teachers. I felt beside myself with joy on Monday morning and talked with great spirit and power on the victory that was coming to our school, using Isaiah 59:19 for my theme: "When the enemy shall come in like a flood, the Spirit of the Lord shall lift up a standard against him."

During breaks in classes, two of the teachers came in to talk to me. "We're not all going to go out to set the world on fire as you say," the first one said. "I'm a Christian, too, even though I may not be quite as excited about my faith as you are."

Later in the morning, the other teacher came to the library to say almost the same words. I made little response, but inside my heart, I felt that they knew I spoke true words and that neither of them was spiritually ready for that kind of power. It made me realize the truth of my insight about Esther—I must bide my time. The Lord was at work, and marvelous would be the results!

Two more years passed, with hope constantly rising and falling in my heart. I worked with the conference temperance leader to help our youth lead a stop-smoking seminar. The Bible teacher and I sponsored our young people in several Revelation seminars. My friend Erleen and I used some of the youth in presenting a Weimar health seminar in the Edmond church. In each of these outreaches, I expected spiritual renewal. God richly blessed our efforts, but the great revival eluded us every time.

Then came a visit after school in April that temporarily blasted my dreams. The superintendent of education from the Oklahoma Conference office came to see me in the library. "There's little support for you on our Parkview board," he said. "It's in your best interest to accept a teaching position in one of our one-room schools."

Stunned, I ignored the thrust of his words to quickly respond, "Oh, I can't think of going from this school. I've set myself to make a revival take place on this campus, and I plan to stay until it takes place."

"The Holy Spirit is in charge of touching hearts," he calmly replied. "God doesn't need you or any other specific person to make for such a happening."

His words fell on deaf ears as I continued to defend myself. "I've held the love and power of God before these youth for eight years. It would be a defeat for me to leave."

"You're a spiritually strong person, Donna, but you have trouble controlling young people. There are many complaints that you allow them to get by without completing their work. You're far too sympathetic to work with these modern youth. Worldly influences aren't quite so strong among the children in our small schools."

I lost control and began to cry. "I know I'm too easy on the young people, but they surely learn something from me. I have an obligation to them for the fulfillment of my prayers."

He continued to reason with me, and then finally stood to leave. "Think about what I've suggested to you when you get home this evening," he said. "I believe you'll understand that I have your best interest in mind." He prayed for me and left.

I sat bewildered. It seemed unbelievable that the board really wanted me to leave Parkview. My discipline left a lot to be desired, but surely I had good points that made up for that weakness.

Then I knelt to pray. "Jesus, remember all my prayers

for You to move upon these youth. I know most people think I'm a dreamer. They don't think my prayers could make anything spectacular happen, but I know they can. You have all power, and I have claimed Your own promises. I haven't presumptuously sought for these blessings. It's for Your sake that You must do something. What would happen to the faith of these young people if You moved me away without proving that my prayers were answered?"

Again, my God didn't see fit to intervene. When the word came that the Parkview board didn't rehire me, I accepted a teaching position at the one-room school in Lawton.

Because of the encouragement of the education superintendent, I felt certain that I could find success in this new teaching situation. But my overly compassionate nature brought the same difficulty. I found it almost impossible to keep the eight children of varying ages under control. To complicate matters, my mother became very ill at the beginning of the school term, and I felt compelled to spend every weekend with her, making it impossible to be active in the church.

Following her death in February, I made a decision that totally changed my life. Mother had left a comfortable home in the small town of Thomas, and a small income for each of her children. After nine years in church schools with no apparent success in bringing revival plus constant problems in teaching, I determined to move to her home to promote a deeper walk with God through writing. I could supplement my income by doing substitute teaching in the Thomas public schools. Perhaps I could exert more influence with written words promoting God's way than in teaching young people. With the permission of my brother and two sisters, I moved to my mother's home at the close of the school term to follow my dream.

20

Waiting

With great anticipation, I now began life in the small town of Thomas. The school usually called me one or two days each week to fill in for an absent teacher, but otherwise, I enjoyed freedom from regular work. When I drove eighteen miles to Weatherford to attend church, I passed the road that led to Duane's house. The Oklahoma State Department of Education had transferred his work to western Oklahoma, so he and his wife now lived in that city. Sometimes a brief prayer ran through my mind when I crossed the road on Sabbath: "Make Duane remember that today is Your day that he should keep holy." In spite of a lingering faith that our home would one day be restored, I seldom thought of him.

The apathy of my family and of believers and unbelievers alike made me burn to reveal the loveliness of Jesus. I led in a health seminar at church and in a prophecy seminar in my home, taught Sabbath School, spoke occasionally for church services, and visited door-to-door. In every activity, I tried to exalt Jesus' life. I also put forth earnest efforts in writing. Publishers said "no" to my book idea and rejected every magazine article, but I remained positive. Since I walked with the Lord in a close relationship, I trusted that He would soon enable me to win souls and write words to encourage His people.

Added blessings, brought by my freedom from teaching, were frequent visits to my daughters' homes—Lori and Vonda, who had both married and lived in Loma Linda, and Tami, who was engaged. On July 23, 1991, the call came from Vonda's husband announcing the birth of my first grandchild. "She was born at 10:30 this morning and weighs only four pounds," he cried. "Her arm is crooked, which the doctor says can be corrected, but he's afraid of many other problems—her lungs and heart are undeveloped, and the shape of her head appears abnormal. We've named her Ciara." He ended with a sob.

Desperately desiring my first grandchild to be perfect, I spoke words of reassurance: "The medical profession can perform miracles today. Surely there isn't anything wrong they can't make right. And sometimes doctors paint bleak pictures. Don't believe a word he tells you until you know the facts. Could Vonda talk to me?"

He handed the phone to Vonda. I tried to console and encourage my grief-stricken daughter, but she seemed too dazed to respond. Promising her I would stay in prayer, I said goodbye.

I dropped to my knees to make demands to my heavenly Father. "This baby must be healthy. All the babies born to my siblings' children are hale and hearty. We're Your special people—You can't allow a damaged child to be born to us."

I refused to believe the baby could be afflicted and constantly looked heavenward to plead, "Father, make the tests prove Ciara to be healthy."

It was comforting to know that Lori and her husband sat with Vonda and Roy at the hospital. Wednesday morning, she called with a dreadful diagnosis. "The doctor says she has multiple congenital deformities, a tumor on her brain, nasal passage problems, heart problems, and hip and jaw deformity. They give no hope for her life but plan to keep her alive on a breathing machine and feeding tubes while they run tests."

"How are Vonda and Roy taking this awful news?"

"They're heartsick, Mom. They need you here."

"I'll come as soon as I can get a ticket." My optimistic nature came fully to life. The heavenly Father had performed many miracles in answer to prayer in my fifteen years of walking with Him. My granddaughter would be the next marvel from His hands. As I filled a small bottle with olive oil, I made a plan: "I'm going to fast and pray all the way to California. When I get there, I'll anoint my grandchild and pray that God will heal her."

During the 1,200 miles of highway on the Greyhound bus, I hardly felt hungry as I talked to the Lord about Ciara. My faith remained strong that I could expect restoration for my granddaughter.

Mile after mile, I pondered God's will. How could He allow me to dream such big dreams that didn't come true in spite of earnest prayer? I had thought Duane's conversion and return would bring the answer. When that didn't occur, I became positive that there would be a revival at Parkview. After being forced to leave the school,

I expected a heavenly move at Lawton, but there the situation became even worse. No special success had attended my two years' work in Thomas. It all seemed so mysterious. As I clasped my small bottle of olive oil, I dared to dream that the healing of my granddaughter might begin the outpouring of heavenly blessings.

Twenty-eight hours later, at midnight, I sat in a rocking chair in the Kaiser Hospital Neonatal Intensive Care Unit, where the nurse took tiny Ciara from her incubator and placed her in my arms. I loved her from the moment I laid eyes on her. She was hooked to an I.V. and a heart monitor. In a room containing several babies who were of normal size and normal looks, my granddaughter, with her deformed arm and long, slim body seemed the most precious of all. I marveled at the beauty of her sweet, miniature face. Since I had fasted, prayed, and believed for divine healing, I couldn't resist putting my finger on the olive oil and rubbing her hand, arm, and body while I whispered a simple prayer, but my faith vanished and my fast ended before the reality of her deformities.

The next day Ciara's nurse led Roy, Vonda, and me into an office. Soon Dr. Swarner came, looked at our somber faces, and gave us his report and recommendation.

"I'm sorry to bring you this kind of news," he began. "Ciara is a Trisomy 18 baby, which means that her eighteenth chromosome is abnormal. Her many problems indicate she can't live more than a few days without the breathing machine, so I suggest we stop life support and let Mother Nature take her course. Trisomy 18 babies can never walk or talk, thus giving no opportunity for a quality life. After we make sure she can eat, we'll remove all tubes, and you're free to take her. Do you agree with that decision?"

The doctor's words proved too much for Vonda. Even as we nodded assent, she burst into tears. Roy hugged her close and tried to comfort her. "Don't cry, honey. We'll take her home and hope to have a few days with her." Then turning to the doctor, he said, "Take away the life support. We'll face whatever the future brings."

One day later, we left the hospital with the proud daddy carrying Ciara to the car. She had wound herself around our hearts, and all of us were silently praying, "Please give us just a little time with her, Jesus."

She was now one week old and weighed only three and one-half pounds. Her delicate condition led us to hold her almost constantly. Two or three times in the next week, she seemed to be dying. We watched as she turned blue, then suddenly revived. Calls to the doctor made us aware that we should expect her death at any moment. Unbelievably, she passed each crisis, and we thanked God for another day.

She continued to live in spite of the doctor's predictions, turning my two weeks in California into an extended stay. I couldn't leave my children with the responsibility of this fragile baby. No way would any of us consider placing her in an institution.

At six weeks, she let out a terrifying scream, bringing Vonda and me immediately to her crib. We could see nothing wrong except that she seemed blue. The same afternoon, while she was in my arms, I noticed that she had quit breathing. In a few seconds she caught her breath, then again uttered a heart-rending cry. From that day, her breathing disorder was full-blown. If we watched, we learned that a quick massage of her chest would start her breath and prevent the ordeal.

"Mom, she's not breathing!" Often in the ensuing weeks I heard that call from my daughter. Vonda was much more efficient than I in keeping Ciara breathing. I tried to watch her carefully but often became distracted. Since the baby required constant attention, one of us held her while the other did the cooking, cleaning, and other household activities, and we took turns attending church on Sabbath morning.

Weeks passed, and Ciara prospered in spite of breathing difficulties and several sicknesses. Antibiotics helped her recover from illness, but every time the doctor examined her, he gave us the same diagnosis: "This looks like the end. Be prepared for her death." She always bounced back. We recognized it as the power of the love she received from her keepers. When she was about six months old, she responded to us with a beautiful smile. From that day, we loved to bring that grin to her face. The doctor said she could never talk or walk, but our Trisomy 18 baby controlled the household with only her upturned lips.

On a walk home from the Campus Hill Seventh-day Adventist church one Sabbath morning, I overtook a white-haired woman with a Bible in her hand. "You must be a Seventh-day Adventist?" I asked.

"Yes, I'm on my way home from church. I live only a few blocks away."

Thus began a friendship with a fellow believer who lived within walking distance of my children's home.

Alice and I talked on the telephone every day, always ending our conversation with prayer, and she sometimes came to visit. After we became good friends, she decided to enlighten me about Ciara. "Your attention keeps this child alive. No way would she live long if you didn't keep her breathing when she has these spells." She looked at Ciara as I cradled the infant in my arms.

"You're right. Our attention to this breathing disorder helps, but she's also a symbol of the power of love. The doctor tells us constantly that she can't live, but Ciara seems determined to prove him wrong. She basks in the love and attention we give her."

"I hate to sound heartless, but it seems that there are so many needy ones to whom you could minister if you weren't bound to this one child."

You have no idea how I love her," I quickly responded. "The heavenly Father has used a handicapped child to send this 'Moses' to the wilderness to learn about Him. Everyone looks at this little baby as worthless. Before she came into my life, I regarded such children as useless. But Jesus considers her of such value that He would have died for only her. Her weak, pitiful life symbolizes souls lost in sin. Just as our love and attention sustain her life when the doctor tells us constantly that she's going to die, so the love of Jesus uplifts doomed human beings from the pit of sin."

Ciara whimpered in discontent, and I shifted her in my arms so I could bounce her. "This baby has brought healing to my heart," I continued. "Caring for her has completely quenched my desire for my ex-husband to come back to me. Sometimes I'm amazed when I realize I'm so satisfied alone; however, the earnest prayers I've prayed and my disappointment that he didn't return make for a grand appointment for a spiritual victory."

"How can you have a spiritual victory when you do so little in the church?" Alice looked at me with questioning eyes. "You don't teach Sabbath School. You no longer work with young people. You don't present programs. Your musical ability lies dormant."

"Only God knows the answer to that question. I've always been active in church work and in community service, but the Lord has taken me from a busy life to tend one little lamb. When my training is complete, He will fulfill His plan. Today I'm shut away from the world and all its problems, but I'm not cut off from God. You should see me carry this little darling back and forth across the living room floor every morning while I quote Scripture and pray. This time with my Lord carries me victoriously through every day."

I knew Alice didn't understand. None of our family or friends could comprehend our dedication to Ciara. I saw her value, even as God sees worth in the lowliest soul. Whatever the future held, I planned to take care of her. I praised the Lord daily for the picture she gave me of His love.

Ciara got very sick on January 2, 1993 when she was 17-1/2 months old. Again we took her to the doctor to hear the same report: "I doubt if she makes it this time." He gave her an antibiotic, which seemed to help, but then her condition worsened. Vonda and I stayed with her night and day. I sat in the rocker holding her on a Monday morning after she had kept us up all night. Vonda sat on the divan. "Do you think she's going to live, Mom?"

"Oh yes! She's come through sicknesses every time, even when the doctor says she can't make it. She'll pull through this time." Turning to Ciara, I noticed she had quit breathing. As usual, I briskly rubbed her chest, commanding, "Ciara, breathe, baby!" Vonda got up from the divan to stand beside me. Ciara did not catch her breath. Sadness overwhelmed me as Vonda spoke the words of finality, "She's dying." She died an easy death in my arms, making no struggle, but simply going to sleep in Jesus. We cried through her funeral service in Azure Hills Seventh-day Adventist Church; then flew with her to Oklahoma to bury her beside Duane's father in a rustic cemetery close to Thomas.

In response to my children's request, I stayed in California several weeks longer while they adjusted to life without Ciara; then I returned to Oklahoma with a heart bursting with hope. After a twenty-month interlude, I felt on the verge of success. The girls and their husbands bought me a computer, and with zeal and fervor I sat at this modern machine to pursue writing, determined to call God's people to revival.

21

The Exceeding Abundant Answer

I stood praying in a special place at the edge of Thomas early one morning, when the Lord gave me a heartbreaking picture of Himself on Calvary. My heart burned with the pain of the cross—the reality of each sin of the whole human family being placed on Jesus. I could hardly bear the magnitude of the Saviour's anguish, yet multitudes go their way without a care, making a waste of a priceless treasure.

For the several minutes that the picture stayed in my mind, tears streamed down my face while I cried out to heaven, "Jesus, You went through this horror for me and the whole human race. If only I could make my people know the price You paid, it would transform us into disciples who again would turn this world upside down."

I went home to write in my prayer journal:

April 4, 1994

Again, dear Saviour, I present the condition of Your people to You. You have paid this awful cost to buy back from Satan every human being in the world. Something must be done to melt and subdue stubborn hearts. How can I show Your people that the most valuable possession anyone can own is You?

This is the work You have performed in me—a seemingly impossible feat. My dearest treasure was the only man I ever loved, he was my knight in shining armor and reigned as king on the throne of my heart. He was the head of my house, the father of my children, and my best friend. I loved him intensely. I sent him to work with a kiss every morning and couldn't wait for him to return in the evening.

How did You do it, Father? How did You take such an idol from me and make Yourself my only love? The answer to that question lies in the power of Your Word that I hid in my heart. The memorized Word taught me to care for You. The Word urged me on to a better life. The vision of what I could become if I were totally committed to You became more real every day, and I desired that life with all my heart. I heard Your voice, I obeyed Your commands, and I learned to love You more and more.

The strange thing is that the more I loved You, the more I loved my husband. I continued to read and memorize the promises of the little Book, which were sweet as honey to my mouth, but turned bitter in my belly time after time as my fondest dreams were shattered. The hope I found in those promises enabled You to work mightily in my life to give me an eye single to Your glory. The day came, and I can't pinpoint the time, when You took from me a man I thought I couldn't live without, then You possessed me and became the Man I truly can't live without. I go to bed at night and wake up in the morning thinking about my love affair with You, my blessed Saviour, and how I can win everyone out there to the same experience.

Constantly Satan is trying to put it on me that I'm a dreamer—no way are You going to perform the miracle I'm expecting. As I look at my family, the members of our churches, and this world, it looks impossible. But in my study this week I was led to Genesis 18:14, where You said, "Is anything too hard for the Lord? At the time appointed I will return unto thee. . . ."

You have an appointed time when You are going to respond to my prayers of all these years. The promises I hold before You are for bigger miracles than parting the Red Sea. I claim Your promise for revival and reformation. I claim Your promise to save Your people. Most of all I claim the Holy Spirit in one-hundred times more power, one-hundred times more wisdom, and to bring an intense love for Jesus.

Your chosen time is upon us. You have moved from leading us to the Red Sea to standing behind us in order to blind Satan to the great work You are getting ready to do.

"Because the Lord loved you and because He

would keep the oath which He had sworn unto your fathers, hath the Lord brought you out with a mighty hand and redeemed you out of the house of bondmen, from the hand of Pharaoh, king of Egypt" [Deuteronomy 7:8].

I know that Your one-hundred-fold blessing for giving up our home for Your sake is soon coming. I will not stray from Your side!

I love you,

Donna

Little did I know that even as I wrote my journal prayer, my God was making a way for a miraculous answer. It began in August of that same year with a visit.

"Why do you carry those cards with you?" I pointed to a set of ringed cards lying on a chair beside Dottie LeFore as we sat on my screened-in back porch eating. Our acquaintance had begun in California when she introduced herself to me as a third cousin on my grandmother's side of the family, making me happily aware that I had relatives in the Adventist church. Since Dottie had served time as a missionary in Africa and now made door-to-door witnessing her major work for the Lord, I had immediately been drawn to her religious zeal. She had come for a two-week visit from her home in Oregon.

"These are my memorizing cards, which I keep with me at all times so I can learn during any free moment. Listen to this verse which I started learning while I waited for you to bring my breakfast: 'And, behold, I have given the children of Levi all the tenth in Israel for an inherit-

The Exceeding Abundant Answer 197

ance...'" Leviticus 18:21. She quoted the verse with an air of confidence, then took a bite of my homemade bread, which I had toasted to eat with oatmeal bake and fruit for our first meal of the day. "I've written four verses on each card for sixteen doctrinal studies," she explained. "We must be able to defend our faith. 'None but those who have fortified the mind with the truths of the Bible will stand through the last great conflict'" *The Great Controversy,* page 593.

"I've memorized for years, but it's never occurred to me to learn our beliefs," I responded. "I doubt I could quote very many verses backing the sanctuary message, the mark of the beast, or tithing, as you just repeated. And I know we should be able to back every doctrine with Scripture."

"Our Bibles may be taken in the days ahead, but no one can take verses from our minds," Dottie replied.

"You've inspired me to make a set of cards for myself. I could also include memorizing doctrine in my work with the youth in my church. We must get ready for the time of trouble that's fast approaching, and we need to do everything possible to prepare our people. Now, I hate to change the subject, but let's put these dishes in the sink and go to my computer. After five years of practice, my first success in writing is going to the press next week. I want you to help me proof what I've written."

"I'd love to be a critic for the debut of a writer, but what kind of writing is this?"

"Larry Adler, the editor of *The Weatherford Daily News,* has agreed to let me write a health column for his newspaper." I turned on my computer and brought up the health directory. "I call my discourse '*Nature's Way.*'

Each letter of the title forms an acronym to remember the eight natural remedies, the subject matter of my articles: N = Nutrition, A = Air, T = Temperance, U = Unpolluted Water, R = Rest, E = Exercise, S = Sunshine, and Way = God's Way—the only way to health and happiness. I'll receive no money, but I'm elated at the privilege of presenting a total-vegetarian lifestyle to the 5,000 people who receive this newspaper."

"I can imagine your writing such information in my part of the world where apples are grown, but this is cattle country. What will these Oklahoma farmers say when you write derogatory statements about using their animal products for food?"

"It seems likely that I could meet resistance, but the Lord has opened the door for me. I'll pray He'll stop opposition and use *'Nature's Way'* to open hearts to His truth."

Dottie and I went through my writing sentence by sentence. She gave me several pointers for improvement. Then in the days ahead, she helped me prepare features on two more subjects—"drinking water" and "exercise."

After Dottie returned to Oregon, I went back to my computer with two writing projects—the first, my health column, and the second, the compilation of doctrinal memory cards to learn our message. At first, I had no thought except to make memory cards for myself and for my youth class at church, but as I continued work, my ideas enlarged. Why not add Spirit of Prophecy quotations and first-letter helps—two extras I had practiced? Why not produce the cards for every Adventist? Scripture memory had been powerful in my life—perhaps it could bring the long-prayed-for revival. Excitement coursed through my body at the thought.

A better job than substitute teaching came my way, giving me more time to write. I became a night caretaker for a 93-year-old woman who had taught me in eighth grade. She paid me to sleep at her house. The salary I earned from Melva, plus my income from the estate, allowed me to live quite comfortably, while with all my heart I pursued writing.

After a few months of work, my telephone bill began to mount with calls for advice to an old friend, Sharon Nottingham, who lived in Plano, Texas. She became invaluable to me as I mailed lessons to her and asked for her opinion. Also, Elder James Hayward read through my studies and made several suggestions for verses and quotations.

Finally, in May of 1996, after twenty months of work, I picked up one hundred copies of *Sealing Touch* from the printer in Weatherford. With an expectant heart, I collated the cards, snapped a ring in the corner holes and sent copies to my daughters and several close friends. Their positive response led me to ask permission to make a presentation at a women's retreat at Wewoka Woods Adventist Center at the end of the month. To my amazement, I sold thirty sets to a group of fifty women, who gave thrilling comments: "This is a great idea!" "We should have been learning our message ages ago!" "God has given you this ministry to call us back to His Word."

I went home to telephone the good news to my daughters. "The Lord blessed me abundantly last night as I shared the power of Scripture memory with a group of women who seemed to believe every word. I'm so happy that I'm walking on clouds. Promoting memorizing, the very activity that saved me, is going to enable us to do the great work we've always dreamed about."

Tami immediately went to a leader of the church in Keene to set a date for me to present my plan. I ordered a thousand sets of memory cards from the Weatherford printer. When they were printed, I took them to Texas, where Tami and I worked two days collating books. I also went to the college computer department and printed out envelopes with my name and address, along with a $6.00 price tag. Since the presentations would be on Sabbath, the envelopes would allow those who purchased my books to pay me later.

Again, the Lord's hand on me, as I gave a fifteen-minute talk in Sabbath School, made me know that the fulfillment of every dream rested in my new ministry. "Jesus holds His nail-scarred hands before the Heavenly Father in the sanctuary in heaven and prays for us to work in harmony with Him." (See *Review and Herald,* January 28, 1890.) He calls us to His Word for our preparation. "Therefore shall ye lay up these My Words in your heart and in your soul." Deuteronomy 11:18. Jesus knows His Word will convert and cleanse us and send us forth to prepare the world for His coming.

Amazingly, I sold forty sets in the sanctuary and thirty more following my presentation for the young adult Sabbath School class. Tami and I were thrilled. As we walked from the church, Charles and Brenda Bishop caught our attention. Brenda's remarks brought more joy to my heart. "God has raised you up to do a mighty work. Your memorizing plan could revive a lukewarm church. I'm going to write to 3ABN so you can present it on television."

The Exceeding Abundant Answer

"Mom, who would ever have dreamed that this is the answer God had for you all those years you prayed to do a work for Jesus?" Tami asked. "It's almost too good to be true."

"I know, honey. I feel as if God has opened heaven to pour out a blessing so big I can hardly contain it."

One week later I called Tami. "I got a letter from a lady in the Keene church giving me a 'Nathan' rebuke. She writes, 'I couldn't wait for my Sabbath School class to be over so I could buy your books. When I got home, I realized that I had lost my Sabbath blessing of the presence of the Lord because of wanting to buy on His holy day. Your books are wonderful, but I don't think you should sell them on the Sabbath. I'm returning the book I picked up.'"

"The woman is being fanatical, Mom. Many people sell their books in the church on Sabbath. When the books are for the spiritual uplifting of God's people, it can't be wrong."

"I've tried to rationalize it away, too, but I don't feel good about it. I think the Lord spoke to me through this woman. Some Christians can get by with selling on Sabbath, but it's clear to me that the Lord doesn't want the memory cards sold on His holy day. I plan to send everyone's money back. I'm thankful I kept a list of all the names and addresses as the checks came in."

The voice of God had touched my heart. Much as I wanted to keep the money to start paying back my big investment, I immediately sent a letter and a refund to each person who had taken my books on the Sabbath in Keene. Then with a clear conscience, I went back to the work of collating the remaining cards. I also returned to the computer to pursue a new idea. Because my memory cards weren't suitable for children younger than ten, I began compiling a children's memorization coloring book with verses from *Sealing Touch*.

A few weeks later on a Sunday night, I stood at a small round table in a corner area of the Adventist Book Center at the Oklahoma camp meeting. "Jesus commands us to 'Hide His Word in our hearts!'" I called out to gain the attention of those who walked by. Many came to the bookstore after the last meeting of the day to shop for books and food.

Soon 14-year-old Angel Golding joined me. Nancy Doshier and I were keeping Angel and three teenage boys in our tent. We had started these young people memorizing the studies in our Wednesday night youth meetings even before I had them printed, so I had asked them to come by the ABC to quote verses to help sales. Now as a young couple came along, I held up my book. "Jesus tells us, 'Let thine heart retain My Words' [Proverbs 4:4]. Do you have time to hear this girl quote a few verses from a lesson in this memory book?"

"Certainly," the man answered. "I love to hear our youth say Bible texts."

Angel immediately repeated the first three verses of the "The Righteousness of Christ" study, giving the text after each verse.

"I'm impressed," the man's wife said. "Let's take two books, John."

"That was fun!" Angel said. "Next time I'll do the last three verses of the same study."

"I'm quite proud of you, my little memorizer." I gave her a big squeeze. "I sold forty-eight sets at the Sunday book sale this morning. Maybe we can sell even more than that in the store, with you and the boys helping me."

I turned to talk to a woman who picked up one of my books. "Jesus tells us, 'Let the Word of Christ dwell in you richly' [Colossians 3:16]. Memorization is both fun and powerful. Do you have time to hear this young lady quote a few verses?"

"How could I refuse such a pretty girl? Of course, I'll listen to you, honey."

As she had planned, Angel spoke the last verses of her study. Her friendly face held the attention of our prospect.

"That was wonderful! But I have a terrible time memorizing. I could never learn verses as you have done."

"Let me show you an easy way," Angel quickly answered, holding out a set of memory cards. "Always pray for help before you begin. That's what Donna tells me to do. Then read only one verse and text two or three times, considering the meaning each time. Now flip the card to the first-letter helps, and read again. From now on, read the verse from the helps page. Soon you can quote it by memory. Then with God's words in your mind, you can meditate on them all day long."

"You've convinced me, honey. I'll give it a try. Please give me three books so I can also give them to my daughters. I know it's important for us to memorize God's Word."

"Angel, I'm going to hire you to be my sales agent. Your presentation is almost impossible to resist."

"I love it! With the next customer, I'll repeat the Spirit of Prophecy quotation from the study."

Angel and I continued our work for one hour until closing time, and then I ran to Sharon's tent. She had driven from Texas to attend camp meeting. "I'm too keyed up to sleep." I spoke quietly so I wouldn't awaken her granddaughters. "We must thank God for the great success He's pouring on my memory cards. Not only do they appeal to adults, but you should have seen Angel's shining face as she quoted verses.

"You and I prayed for revival at Parkview Adventist School, and now the Lord has answered every prayer with this ministry that has potential to revive every youth throughout the world who can be motivated to seriously memorize Scripture. But how can we get these books to our youth and to the world?"

"God has a plan," Sharon assured me. "Listen to this verse from Joel: 'And the Lord shall utter His voice before His army: for His camp is very great: for he is strong that executeth His Word: for the day of the Lord is great and very terrible; and who can abide it?' [Joel 2:11].

"Those words tell me that the work will be finished by God's people executing His Word. God has given you this ministry to be part of that plan. We must patiently wait for His next move. Your success makes me anxious to return home so I can get back to my work of drawing pictures for your new memory coloring book for children. We must complete this book soon to enable the very young to learn the message."

Sharon and I prayed, then I hurried back to my tent to

climb to my top bunk-bed. There I dreamed of an army of memorizing youth "who quickly take the message of a crucified, risen, and soon-coming Saviour to the world." *Messages to Young People,* page 196.

22

A Fulfilled Dream

"May I speak to Larry Adler?" I asked the receptionist at the office of *The Weatherford Daily News*. "He isn't here today," she answered. "Phillip Reid, our owner and publisher, could see you."

She ushered me into Phillip's office, where I immediately presented my case.

"After you printed my article several weeks ago suggesting that a reduction in meat consumption would help to feed a hungry world, you published two editorials critical of my stance. Did the negative response upset you?"

"Not at all," Phillip answered. "We like for people to write editorials. It arouses interest and possibly helped the readership of your piece."

"Then may I ask you why you've stopped publishing my column? It hasn't been in the paper for over two months."

Phillip looked a little sheepish. "Do you remember your discourse on hot dogs printed last May?"

"Oh, yes. I reported that children eating hot dogs once a week experienced twice the brain tumor risk of those who ate none, while those eating hot dogs two times a week experienced a three-times-normal risk. Children who downed twelve hot dogs a month faced 9.5 times the leukemia risk."

"Those were pretty harsh words for Bar S Meat-Packing Plant to read," Phillip said. "They spend lots of money advertising in our newspaper."

My mouth almost dropped open, but I quickly regained my composure. "I understand why Bar S might be upset, but don't you think we have an obligation to inform the world of these studies?"

"Perhaps so, but as the owner and publisher, I have to give consideration to those who promote their products in my newspaper."

"My information came from proven facts printed in *Nutrition Action*, a health letter published by the Center for Science in the Public Interest. *The Elk City Daily News* has been running my column in the women's section every Sunday for the last eighteen months. They don't seem upset with the information I write. Tell me, will you ever publish my column again?"

"I'll have Larry Adler get in touch with you," Phillip answered, evading my question.

After a two-year life span, I knew I had seen the end of *"Nature's Way"* in *The Weatherford Daily News*—a step downward in my health work. But my memory card work became more prosperous every day. I attended a Sabbath School workshop in Texas, where the education superintendent of the Texico Conference saw my memory books and ordered them for every teacher in his schools. "This is exactly what I've been looking for," he said. "I want the young people in my schools to learn our doctrine."

Only a few weeks later, Nancy and I stood near the piano at the front of the Enid church, sharing with Pastor Kornegay after our young people had presented a vespers program.

"I'm impressed with the work you two have done with these youth," Pastor Kornegay said. "The Word is in their minds from this day forward to give them spiritual strength."

"The positive response of your congregation motivated the teens to do well," I replied. "When they heard 'Amen' after every verse, they seemed to put forth more effort."

"Your young people brought a great blessing to all of us. Some of them made five-minute presentations—quite a feat of memory. Whom do I contact to buy the memory cards?"

"I'm the director and chief saleswoman," I answered. "It would please me immensely to leave many books with your people."

An air of excitement enveloped me in the coming months. Daily, I sang praises on my three-mile walk to memorize and pray. "Am I the same woman who mourned the loss of a husband?" I asked the Lord. "I'm so happy that I feel as if I'm in heaven. How I praise You, Father, for being so wonderful to me!"

The phone rang often: "Bring your young people to our church to present the Sabbath morning worship service."

My daughter's recommendation made me a presenter at a women's retreat held in the Wisconsin Dells. To my amazement, seventy women attended my breakaway and bought as many memory cards.

Then came a telephone call that sent my mind into a spin. "This is Dee Hildebrand at 3ABN. Could you come for an interview on '3ABN Presents' on Monday, November 10?"

"I think I could," I answered, while I wondered if I were dreaming. "Let me check with my travel agent, and I'll call you back."

I completely forgot my sixty-two years of age as I jumped up and down in my living room. Another miracle! Evidently Brenda Bishop, whom I had met at the Keene church eighteen months before, had persuaded the 3ABN owners Danny and Linda Shelton to invite me to their program.

A sudden thought sent me back to the telephone to call my good friend. "Sharon, 3ABN called me for an interview. I might get lost trying to get there. Can you go with me?"

"Of course, I'll go with you. Let's meet in Oklahoma City. How could I miss the filming of a show where *Sealing Touch, Jr.*, with pictures drawn by Sharon Nottingham, will be featured?"

The following Sunday, Sharon and I flew together to St. Louis, rented a car, and drove to Thompsonville, Illinois. "Can you believe such a happening?" I asked Sharon as we settled into our quarters. "In my wildest dreams I never thought I might be on television. Now that we're really here, I must confess that I'm nervous."

A Fulfilled Dream   211

"I might get upset if I were being interviewed, but you've always spoken up front. Why are you anxious?"

"It scares me to think that everything I say will be sent across the airwaves. I've messed up in speaking many times. What if I say the wrong words this time? What if I get a crazy expression on my face?"

"Where's your faith, Donna? God gave you this opportunity. We can trust that He won't allow you to fail."

The next morning, I dressed and knelt beside Sharon's bed to hear comforting words. "Put every worry from your mind. The Lord has sent an assurance to me that you will do fine."

Her words helped allay my anxiety. I thanked her for the encouragement. "I know I can trust my heavenly Father, but I'm going on a walk in this gorgeous area behind the house to pray. My memory card ministry belongs to Him, so I'm going to ask Him to put words in my mouth."

Later, we toured the studios, then returned Monday afternoon. In spite of constant prayer, my fast-beating heart and clammy hands spoke of my uneasiness as I looked at the two big cameras with operators standing behind them. Danny and Linda soon came to sit in chairs opposite me. They made a few introductory remarks; then the taping began.

"Look at this book, Linda." Danny turned the pages of *Sealing Touch, Jr.* as he spoke. "It appears to be a typical children's book with poems and pictures, but the titles sound adult: 'The Millennium,' 'The Sabbath,' 'The 2300-Day Prophecy,' 'The Law of God.' Each line of the poem has a picture to color, with a verse to memorize beneath the picture."

"You've taken special verses to teach doctrine to little ones," Linda responded. "It's like taking a satellite seminar and putting it in a book for children."

"Yes, the book has twenty-eight studies, which cover most of our basic doctrines," I said.

"This book, *Sealing Touch*, which is for ages 12 to 112, contains the same studies but has more verses and a longer quotation. I believe all Adventists need to place these studies in their minds to enable them to defend their faith under any circumstances."

"Your books make it possible for every age to learn our message," Danny said.

Then after hearing details of my conversion, he asked, "Have you ever regretted becoming a Seventh-day Adventist?"

"Oh, no! I've told the Lord a thousand times how sorry I am that I waited so long to surrender to Him. I was so involved in my worldly life that it seemed humbling, even fanatical, for me to become a Sabbath-keeper—to attend church while my family went to a football game. Then to my amazement, when I surrendered, darkness turned to such bright light that I felt I could win everybody I knew to my faith. I hadn't listened to anyone in my twenty-year struggle, but I thought I could tell people, and they would listen."

"Did you convert your people?" Linda asked.

"My three girls joined me in the faith within five years, but my big dreams didn't come true. As with most new

A Fulfilled Dream   213

believers, instead of going to the mountaintop, I went to the valley. My home was broken, which brought great heartbreak, but Jesus carried me through victoriously."

Danny and Linda asked questions, and I answered. After thirty minutes, the interview ended. My cup ran over as they assured me that I had done well. I gave them my memory books and thanked them over and over for allowing me to come.

"You worried needlessly—God touched you to give great answers," Sharon said as we drove back to St. Louis to meet our plane. "And remember how you asked me at camp meeting how you could get your memory cards to the world? This interview on 3ABN will blaze your Sealing Touch End-Time Memory Fellowship across the land."

"God is so good to me! I'm ashamed that I ever entertain a doubt about Him. This trip to Thompsonville has been one of the most exciting events of my life. I'm not just happy! I'm ecstatic! And how I thank you for going with me!"

3ABN aired my interview about a week later. The telephone rang all day and continued to ring for almost two weeks. I sold books to individuals, to school teachers, and to Sabbath School teachers. Every call made me realize anew how the Lord had answered my prayers with a ministry promoting an activity with power to revive every sincere seeker. I walked on the mountaintops as I packaged orders and looked forward to the same happening three more times, because 3ABN runs each program four times in a year.

Since my memory book supply was almost diminished,

I ordered upgraded stock with color covers and coil bindings from an Adventist printer in Michigan—Remnant Publications. At the same time, they printed my *Sealing Love* memory cards on the life of Christ.

Calls came for speaking engagements, one of the most exciting being an appointment to be a presenter at the New York Women's Prayer Seminar in the Catskill Mountains in 1998. "You are blessing me beyond my ability to keep up, Jesus," I prayed as I wrote the date on my calendar.

Then came a very special meeting of ASI—Adventist-Laymen's Services and Industries—the following summer, bringing an unbelievable blessing. As I made plans to attend, I called my daughter. "Lori, I'm flying to California to show my memory cards at the ASI convention in Palm Springs this August. I now have three memory books to sell, and with between two and three thousand people expected to attend the convention, sales should pay my expenses. Could you go there with me?"

"Palm Springs is only forty miles from Calimesa," she answered, "so, of course, I'll go. Christy, Nicholas, and Trevor can go with me; then Gary will be free to go on the weekend. You should do well with that kind of crowd."

"It's a big investment, but I've seriously prayed about my decision. Since I don't feel impressed that I shouldn't go, I've sent money to join ASI, rent a booth, and reserve a room in the hotel. With the added expense of an airline ticket, it's going to be an expensive trip to see you if I don't sell."

We set up my booth on Wednesday afternoon. The

A Fulfilled Dream 215

convention began at 7:00 that evening, so I stayed in the booth to sell my cards Wednesday night and all day Thursday. Tami called from her home in Texas on Thursday night after I returned to the hotel room. "Did you do well today, Mom?"

"I sold only twenty sets of memory cards, and I gave a sales pitch to every person who came near. I don't know why the Lord allowed me to spend over a thousand dollars to come here. There's a huge crowd of people, but without a presentation, I really don't expect big sales."

"Do you wish you hadn't gone?" Tami asked.

"I'm glad I came," I answered. "It's been a great experience to see ASI in operation. These Adventist businessmen do a wonderful work for the Lord in every kind of business ministry you can imagine. It's been a good attempt, but I won't do it again."

Friday morning, I went to my booth when the room opened. Several people walked by. Finally, I caught the eye of a young woman with a small boy. "This young man needs to memorize our message," I said as I held my book out to her. She graciously opened a few pages, then closed the book and gave it to me. "We might come back when we have more time." She and the boy walked on.

I felt a small pang but immediately looked down the corridor for other prospective buyers. I didn't have long to wait. A successful-looking man stepped in front of me. "I saw you on 3ABN this morning. Could you show me the Scripture memory cards you told about on the program?"

I could hardly be calm enough to make a presentation

as I realized the third showing of Danny and Linda Shelton's '3ABN Presents' program, with my interview of November 1997, had aired during the ASI meeting, making it possible for every room in the hotel to receive the program. Here stood a man who had seen the show and surely would buy some of my cards. I breathed a prayer of thankfulness, then began: "I have three memorizing plans." I handed him the *Sealing Touch* and the *Sealing Touch, Jr.* memory books. "Every Seventh-day Adventist, young and old, needs to know the basic doctrines outlined in these cards. Ellen White counsels, 'If God has ever spoken by me, the time will come when we shall be brought before councils and before thousands for His name's sake, and each one will have to give the reason of his faith.'"*Last Day Events*, page 209.

The man looked carefully at the two books, then laid them on the table in front of me as I handed him a copy of the *Sealing Love* memory cards. "This memory book on the life of Christ prepares us to take 'the last message of mercy to the world, a revelation of His character of love.'" *Christ's Object Lessons,* page 415.

"I understand from your interview that Scripture memory brought you into the faith," the man said.

"Yes!" I burst out. "The Word worked powerfully in my life. It will change anyone who seriously begins to learn, because it's like a 'burning fire shut up in the bones.'" Jeremiah 23:29.

"That sounds reasonable, and I do like your plan. I'm Doug Sayles from the Review and Herald Publishing Association, and we want to buy your books to sell to the Adventist Book Centers. I'll call you after the convention ends."

A Fulfilled Dream 217

My heart literally jumped into my throat to hear his words. God had sent two miracles my way—3ABN aired my show at this exact time, and the representative from the Review and Herald had seen the presentation. I bubbled over in exhilaration until Lori finally came so I could share my good news. "Now I know why I felt no qualms about coming. This sale places my memory cards in every Adventist Book Center in the country if the ABC managers can be induced to buy them. What a blessing from our wonderful God!"

"This is almost too good to be true!" Lori exclaimed. "And to think you debated about coming. I'll take care of this booth. You go call Tami and Vonda about this marvelous miracle. They need to know that you may have sold only twenty sets of memory cards, but now you have the potential to sell thousands."

I walked on air the next two days. All I could say was, "Thank You, Father! You're so good to me! I love You! I love You!"

God seemed right beside me as I flew back to Oklahoma. "Father, I fasted and prayed for Duane to come back. I sought You earnestly for revival in my school. Now You've performed a far greater miracle in giving me a ministry to reach out to a whole world. You know so much better than Your pitiful little earthly children. How I thank You for fulfilling Your will and not my own!"

I returned home and to my computer. Calls from the television airing continued for days. I worked on my new memory book, *Sealing Faith*. I booked more presentations. I awakened every morning with purpose flooding my heart so big that I knew the day would not be long enough to accomplish all I felt called to do. With that knowledge, I took a walk to memorize and talk to my God, to thank Him for pouring out immeasurable blessings and to ask Him to enable me to carry out all He wanted me to do.

Epilogue

After a wonderful week together at my home in Oklahoma, I watched my three families drive away to their homes in California, Texas, and Wisconsin. A sense of sadness touched my heart to see them go, but I again thanked God for a beautiful family of three couples and ten grandchildren who each attend church every Sabbath—a fulfillment of His promise to bless one-hundredfold those who lose family in this world for His sake. Mark 10:30.

When they were out of sight, I sat down on the porch to meditate a few minutes before beginning my morning walk. Our time together had been an eye-opener for my daughters as I had shared insights with them that have come to me in my senior years. Vonda had started it when she told about a conversation with one of our old friends in Seiling.

"Duane and Donna lived the American dream," the friend had said. "They had everything people long for—togetherness, a wonderful family, and financial success. Since your dad seems to be happily married, has your mom ever regretted her decision to join the church that ruined the relationship?"

Vonda assured her that I am perfectly happy in the Lord. But then she turned to me. "Do you have any regrets, Mom?" she asked.

What Vonda said about my being content in the Lord is certainly true. He has answered a prayer I prayed many times: "Jesus, teach me to love You as I love Duane." He has carried me far beyond my burning love for my man to a love affair with Himself that absorbs my every energy.

And the question Vonda posed to me about regrets? Today, many years later, I'm sad to say that I recognize serious mistakes I made, and I'm very sorry for them.

From childhood, a passionate dream burned within me to do a great work for God. When I fell in love with Duane, this aspiration immediately included him for its fulfillment. My all-consuming zeal to realize this dream blinded me to reality. Because Duane agreed intellectually with the truths I discovered in God's Word, I believed that he knew he must become a Seventh-day Adventist. I was firmly convinced that if I prayed enough, persuaded enough, believed enough, he was certain to join me. I aggressively worked to convince him that he simply *must* unite with me in my dream of shared service. Unwittingly, my zeal may have helped drive him away.

During earlier years in my life, I truly made the best choices I knew to make, but my ardent passion to realize my dream of a great work for God for both Duane and me blinded me to certain realities. I didn't intend to do it, but today I realize that I applied undue pressure to Duane. The approach I used with him, meant to win him to a full conversion to the truth, may have at times actually have made it harder for him to want to join me in my devotion to God and His truth.

Another trait I've been led to recognize is my lack of submission in my prayers—I expected God to answer by granting me exactly what I asked. Yielding my wishes more fully to His will might several times have saved me and the girls much disappointment.

As I look back at how God has led me—especially during the years I "stormed heaven's gates" in prayer concerning Duane, I realize that He had much to teach me about prayer, faith, and submission to His will.

Over and over, I prayed with all the faith I could muster, asking my heavenly Father to intervene on my behalf. I never doubted that He would answer my prayer and give me what I asked. I fasted, I prayed earnestly, I even told the girls and my students in advance exactly how God would answer my prayer.

I told God that He simply *must* not allow my husband to leave me. But my husband did. Then I told God that He simply *must* not allow my husband to pursue a serious romantic relationship with another woman. But my husband did. Finally, I told God that He simply *must* not allow my husband to remarry. But my husband did.

Through bitter disappointment, I've learned that all my prayer and fasting and believing does not obligate or coerce God into yielding to my will. For those of us who have strong wills—and that includes most of us—discovering that we can't ever tell God what He "simply must" do is a hard lesson to learn. The only thing that God simply must do is carry out His own will. And I've learned that when I assume that my will is surely His will, I may be wrong and end up deeply disappointed. And I've learned too that it's not for me to persuade God—even through sincerity and pleading and believing and fasting—to yield to my will. Instead, it's for me to yield to His will.

So it comes down to the difference between what I want and *think* is right—and what God wants and *knows* is right. And when God's will hurts or disappoints or seems impossible to understand, it's often a great test of faith. But I've learned that real faith isn't expecting that God will answer me with just what I ask—it's trusting that God is right and knows what He's doing, even when I can't understand His ways and His answers disappoint me.

I can't blame myself for past mistakes. I must go forward. Besides, I don't know what Duane would have done if I had been a wife who could have taken a stand for the Lord while giving him perfect freedom. He might have remained a Methodist, yet continued to live with me. He might have become a Seventh-day Adventist. Or he might have chosen the same path he's walking today.

Thank God that He is a God well able—both through us, and sometimes in spite of us—to win others to Himself. His dream is to save all of us. He's not willing that any of us should perish, but that we all should come to Him and be saved. That includes me, my three girls and their families, and Duane and his family.

In spite of the many mistakes I've made, I praise Him every day for His leading in my life. Without His divine intervention, which moved me to memorize His Word, I would still be bound to the sweet, good life we lived, or to the "American dream," as our friend called it. I would be longing to live in perfect obedience to the Lord, but I probably would have died with that desire still burning in my breast.

As I began to memorize Scripture, I was miraculously converted. The words I learned gave me zeal for the work and steadily increasing affection for the Lord, until the Word finally carried me past Duane to intense love for Jesus only. Not that I won't always love Duane, but today my love for my Lord is all-sufficient for me.

For years I had placed Duane above the Lord. I truly believe that to idolize a person is one of the most addictive of all sins. Just as the memorized Word gave me victory over putting a man first in my heart, in the place only God should have, so the Word will cleanse hearts of any wrongdoing and pour love for Jesus into those same hearts. Soon the memorizer can say, even as I can testify, "I love Him! I love Him! He's all I want or need!"

I don't want to play down my experience to make anyone think they should practice less faith and pray weaker prayers than I did. I believe God wants all of us to pray earnestly and with perfect faith, but only for those promises that are literally spelled out in His Word. We simply can't move His arm for the selfish desires of our hearts, and especially not when those desires interfere with the free choice He gives all His children. In spite of my presumptuous faith and presumptuous prayers for Duane and for revival in my school and church, I praise God daily that He found a way for me to realize the dream He placed in my heart in an exceeding abundant manner above all that I could ask or think.

So much for reviewing the past, I thought to myself. I needed time with Jesus in His Word. I picked up my memory cards and headed east on my regular walking route. A prayer rose to my lips as I looked at the eastern sky glowing with the brightness of the rising sun. "Soon that sky will shine with Your beauty, dear Saviour. How I long for that glorious day when there will be no more goodbyes, but we will be together forever with You!

"I thank You for this time with my darling children. My love for them and my desire for each of them to live fully for You help me know more of Your feelings. You look down at Your world of more than six billion people with infinite longing for each one to love You. And You endure the pain of a broken heart for each one who rejects You.

"I thank You for the suffering experience You've led me through that has given me a picture of Your anguish. I remember the pain of a broken heart—a horrible, piercing ache for which there's no relief. And that's the pain You've endured for six thousand years. You took my pain away, dear Lord. I want to end Your suffering.

"Make me eloquent to challenge more people to hide Your Word in their hearts, so they can learn to love You. Give me wisdom to compile more memory plans. The Word transforms every life, then multiplies through their lives to feed earth's starving billions. You rejoice over every saved soul. Anoint me and all others who love You to go forth to execute the Word that finishes the work, so You can come."

Epilogue

As I turned the corner to walk north, I opened one of my memory books to review my daily study, with my heart overflowing with gratitude. When I was only 8 years old, I had dreamed of being an "Elsie Dinsmore" in my community—a girl who kept Sunday and who walked closely with Jesus. Now many years later, I *am* an "Elsie"—a woman who keeps Sabbath and carries cards to memorize Scripture. Happiness welled up in my heart.

"You've given me such purpose that I must not waste one minute with a negative thought or regret," I prayed. "Fill my mind with Your Word as we walk together, Jesus, and then I'll return to the fulfillment of my great work for You!"

Seal Your Heart to Jesus With Scripture Memory!

DISCOVER THE AWESOME POWER OF THE MEMORIZED WORD OF GOD!

On the following pages, SEALING TOUCH brings you information about exciting aids to memorizing Scripture available *NOW*— and how to order them.

Sealing Touch
and
Sealing Touch, Jr.

Sealing Touch

❏ 28 doctrinal studies
❏ Coil-bound 4 x 6 cards
❏ Full-color cover
❏ 8-10 KJV verses per study
❏ First-letter helps
❏ Inspiring quote for each study

Sealing Touch, Jr.

❏ 28 doctrinal studies
❏ For children up to 12 years old
❏ Coil-bound 5 x 8 cards
❏ Full-color cover
❏ 4 KJV verses per study
❏ First-letter helps
❏ Inspiring quote for each study
❏ Poem with each study
❏ A picture to color with each verse and quote

Pricing and ordering information on page 231.

Sealing Love
and
Sealing Love, Jr.

Sealing Love

- ❏ 30 studies on Jesus' life
- ❏ Coil-bound 4 x 6 cards
- ❏ Full-color cover
- ❏ 10-16 KJV verses per study
- ❏ First-letter helps
- ❏ Inspiring quote for each study

Sealing Love, Jr.

- ❏ 30 studies on Jesus' life
- ❏ For children up to 12 years old
- ❏ Coil-bound 5 x 8 cards
- ❏ Full-color cover
- ❏ 4 KJV verses per study
- ❏ First-letter helps
- ❏ Inspiring quote for each study
- ❏ Poem with each study
- ❏ A picture to color with each verse and quote

Pricing and ordering information on page 231.

Sealing Faith

Sealing Faith

- ❏ 30 studies from the Old Testament
- ❏ Coil-bound 4 x 6 cards
- ❏ Full-color cover
- ❏ 11-18 KJV verses per study
- ❏ First-letter helps
- ❏ Inspiring quote for each study

Pricing and ordering information on facing page.

Pricing and Ordering Information

Prices:

Sealing Touch $9.95
Sealing Touch, Jr. $11.95
Sealing Love $9.95
Sealing Love, Jr. $11.95
Sealing Faith $9.95

Shipping and handling: $2.00 for one book, $.50 additional. Oklahoma residents add 8 percent sales tax to total order.

You may write, phone, or e-mail your order!

Write to:

Sealing Touch
P.O. Box 314
Thomas, OK 73669

Call:

(580) 661-3837
(Ask about special prices for groups)

E-mail:

sealingtouch@pldi.net

You may also order through any Adventist Book Center.

Contact Donna Nicholas, author of this book and compiler of the memory-card books, at the address, phone, or e-mail above for information about Scripture Memory Seminars.

Visit the Sealing Touch website at:

www.sealingtouch.org